GUNS

IN AMERICAN LIFE

GUNS
IN AMERICAN LIFE

JERVIS ANDERSON

RANDOM HOUSE NEW YORK

Library of Congress Cataloging in Publication Data

Anderson, Jervis.
Guns in American life.

Includes index.
1: Firearms—Social aspects—United States.
I. Title.
TS533.2.A54   1984   306'.46   83-43195
ISBN 0-394-53598-7

Manufactured in the United States of America
24689753
First Edition

TO MAXINE GREENE
A BELOVED TEACHER AND FRIEND

CONTENTS

PART I   An American Institution ι 1
PART II   The Handgun: Romance and Tragedy ι 43
PART III   Rights in Conflict ι 73

PART I

AN AMERICAN INSTITUTION

1

IN JANUARY OF 1981, a few days before his inauguration, Ronald Reagan made his first visit to a foreign leader since his election. From his home state of California he flew to the city of Juarez—just across the border from Texas—for a meeting with José Lopez Portillo, the President of Mexico. According to one of the President-elect's aides, the purpose of the visit was to "set the tone for friendly relations"; and to help mark his entrance upon the international stage Mr. Reagan took along a present for his host—a Remington rifle. The gift of a weapon could have been meant to symbolize Mr. Reagan's sense of what the style of his presidency would be, and, since the presentation was photographed for the newspapers back home, it could also have been intended to reassure those voters who had elected him to provide the nation with a tougher and more decisive leadership than Jimmy Carter's. Millions of Americans had come to believe that the United States needed a more "American" President than Carter—one who could better represent not necessarily the trigger-happy but the trigger-ready side of the nation's character. And what better way was there to symbolize the beginning of an aggressive, no-nonsense presidency than by the token of good relations, a kind of "peacemaker," which the newly elected Chief Executive took with him to Mexico? Moreover, Mr. Reagan was widely admired within the nation's gun-owning community, and if he had not had its support, he might not have been elected so overwhelmingly. To its members he seemed more likely than any President in recent memory to represent and defend what they regard as their constitutional right "to keep and bear arms"—to own as many guns as they want and to use them in whatever legal manner they please. It is plausible to suppose that the wide readership of the nation's gun-and-hunting press voted solidly for him, including the readers of *Pistolero,* a magazine of idiosyncratic outlook that claims to be published "For Americans who believe that God, Guns & Guts Made US Great!" The President is himself, of course, an admirer of guns, and though he's not a hunter he favors the practice of trophy hunting, or shooting animals for sport. "Trophy hunting," he told *Field and Stream* magazine in 1980— echoing a view that prevails within the hunting community—"is a form of harvesting." He added, "I like to shoot, and have done my share of varmint shooting on the ranch. I am not much of a hunter, but I believe I would enjoy it more if I were going to use the meat." The powerful and influential National Rifle Association counts him among its members, and takes credit for delivering millions of the votes that elected him. He is the first candidate for President the N.R.A. has ever endorsed. *Reports from Washington* (an N.R.A. publication that has since changed its name to *Monitor*) stated in November of 1980: "The political clout of the nation's gun owners and sportsmen was clearly evident in the final outcome of the November election. In addition to the landslide victory for President-elect Reagan, the first presidential contender to receive an N.R.A. endorsement in the organization's history, pro-gun candidates were swept into office in Senate and House races."

Mr. Reagan is, however, not the first President to be associated with the N.R.A. or to be identified with the use of guns. A number of Presidents were former soldiers. Andrew Jackson has been called "the dean of duellists" and America's "most violent President." Abraham Lincoln was a decent marksman while growing up on the frontier. Theodore Roosevelt, perhaps the greatest gun enthusiast to have lived in the White House (Mark Hanna once referred to him as "that damned cowboy"), was a member of the N.R.A., and so were Taft, Eisenhower, Kennedy, and Nixon. What distinguishes Reagan is that, as the first presidential candidate to have been endorsed by the N.R.A., he is the first occupant of the White House to be formally linked to the gun lobby's fight against most efforts to regulate the civilian ownership and use of firearms.

There's an irony of some interest in all this. In almost no other part of the world are civilians as free to own and use guns as they are in America, and no major office anywhere has lost so many of its occupants to civilian gunfire as the presidency of the United States; nor have the occupants of any similar office been shot at so frequently by the citizens of their own nation. In 1835, Richard Lawrence attempted to kill Andrew Jackson in Washington; luckily, for the target, his pistols misfired.

In 1865, John Wilkes Booth murdered Abraham Lincoln at a theater in Washington. In 1881, Charles Guiteau shot James Garfield at a railroad station in Washington, inflicting wounds from which the President did not recover. In 1901, Leon Czolgosz assassinated William McKinley at an exposition in Buffalo. In 1912, John Schrank shot and wounded Theodore Roosevelt during a campaign visit that the former President and then Bull Moose candidate was making to Milwaukee. In 1933, Giuseppe Zangara fired at President-elect Franklin Roosevelt in Miami, narrowly missed, and hit Mayor Anton Cermak, of Chicago; Cermak died from his wounds a few weeks later. In 1950, two Puerto Rican nationalists shot their way into Blair House, intending to kill Harry Truman, but were themselves gunned down before they reached the President. Thirteen years later, Lee Harvey Oswald shot and killed John Kennedy in Dallas. In September of 1975, Lynette Fromme pointed a gun at Gerald Ford in Sacramento, and later that month Sara Jane Moore fired at him in San Francisco. And, most recently, John Hinckley, Jr., shot and seriously wounded Ronald Reagan in the nation's capital.

If President Regan's inclusion in that series of events is more ironic than the others'—in view of his popularity with and support of the pro-gun lobby—the fact doesn't seem to have made much of an impression on him. He has found no reason to change or soften his views on the question of gun ownership—to the great admiration of gunmakers and gun users. "Shooters, generally—at least, handgunners—are fortunate that we have the President we have," Bill Ruger, an executive of Sturm & Ruger, which is one of the nation's larger gun-producing firms, said in a gun publication a few months after Hinckley's attack on Mr. Reagan. A full-page tribute in *Pistolero* applauded the President for refusing to alter his pro-gun position. "THANK GOD FOR PRESIDENT REAGAN, a man who, even after being shot, realizes that more gun controls are not the solution to our crime problem," its text read. "Here's a man of guts, common sense and vision. May he live to be 120!"

Americans who came of age during the past two decades or so are probably the first generation in the country's history to have grown up amid such an epidemic of gun attacks on the presidency, and also on such prominent national figures as Robert Kennedy, Martin Luther King, Jr., Malcolm X, George Wallace, Allard Lowenstein, and John Lennon. Shortly after the attempt on President Reagan's life, a reader wrote to *Newsweek:* "If you had told me in 1963 that in the next twenty years I would see one President shot to death, one wounded and one twice threatened by gun-wielding assailants, one senator killed and one wounded and one governor wounded, I would have said, 'You've got to be kidding! That's not the United States, it's a shooting gallery.'" Whether or not the United States is a shooting gallery, it unquestionably accommodates the world's largest and freest gun culture—one whose roots are deep in the nation's past.

2

IN DICKENS' *Martin Chuzzlewit*—based partly on the novelist's first visit to America, in 1842—Chuzzlewit and his "fellow wanderer" Mark Tapley are taken aback by the free and casual use of guns in the United States. In the town of Eden—representing Cairo, Illinois—the two Englishmen make the acquaintance of Hannibal Chollop, who, they discover, usually carries "a brace of revolving pistols in his coat pocket," and who utters boasts like the following: "It ain't long since I shot a man down with that, sir. . . . I shot him down, sir, for asserting . . . that the ancient Athenians went ahead of the present Locofoco Ticket." When Tapley later mentions the "murderous little persuaders" that Chollop carries and is always ready to use, one Mr. Pogram comes heatedly to the defense of his fellow-American. How strange and singular, Pogram exclaims, is "the settled opposition to our Institutions which pervades the British mind." Chuzzlewit can scarcely believe what he has heard. "What an extraordinary people you are!" he replies. "Are pistols . . . and such things Institutions on which you pride yourselves? Are bloody duels, brutal combats, savage assaults, shooting down, and stabbing in the streets, your Institutions?"

Guns and shooting down were American institutions

long before that, and have remained so ever since. "The United States is the only modern industrial urban nation that persists in maintaining a gun culture," the historian Richard Hofstadter wrote in 1970. "It is the only industrial nation in which the possession of rifles, shotguns, and handguns is lawfully prevalent among large numbers of its population." There are now nearly two hundred million civilian-owned guns of every kind in America, and that figure includes some sixty million handguns. In 1980 alone, about two and a half million handguns were made and sold in the United States, and about a quarter-million more were assembled here from imported parts. In the late 1960s, one new handgun was sold in America every twenty-four seconds. Today, demand has doubled: two are sold every twenty-four seconds.

John Hinckley was not raised by a gun-owning family, but some of the views he came to hold and the ease with which he was able to acquire his firearms are typical of the gun culture. Hinckley wanted to commit a "historical deed" with his gun in order to win the affection of a young actress—a frivolous reason compared with, say, John Wilkes Booth's; but the act he committed places him solidly within the history of American gun assassins. He bought his little handgun in a pawnshop, easily and cheaply, just like all the others who have killed or tried to kill public figures. And only a gun culture could have inspired his "Guns Are Fun!," a poem, written before his attack on President Reagan, that begins:

See that living legend over there?
With one little squeeze of the trigger
I can put that person at my feet moaning and groaning
    and pleading with God.
This gun gives me pornographic power.
If I wish, the President will fall and the world will look
    at me in disbelief
All because I own an inexpensive gun.

"The U.S. has preserved for its people the liberty to kill almost at will," said the *Straits Times* of Singapore, which was among the newspapers of the world that looked at Hinckley in disbelief.

It was reported in 1982 that outpatients at a mental-health center in Montana were being taught to use firearms as part of a "life-skills" class program. The students were given .22-caliber rifles, but with a stern warning that the guns were to be used only at the firing range; the therapists didn't want their patients bringing guns inside the mental center. One may wonder what the therapists feared might happen, since they had assured the surrounding community that the patients were harmless—that they "wouldn't hurt a fly." Later that year, the town of Commerce, Georgia, invited members of the World Fast Draw Association to come on down and help celebrate the Fourth of July. The Association obliged, and the Fourth was celebrated in gun-blazing Wild West fashion: good guys and bad guys ("marshal" and "outlaws") staged "shootouts" in the streets of Commerce while men, women, and children looked on and applauded. Also in 1982, a committee of the Kentucky General Assembly approved a bill that would allow members to carry concealed handguns on the floor of the house. (During a free-for-all in that assembly in 1936, a legislator drew his pistol and shot up the skylight of the chamber.) Guns may be dangerous in Detroit—where the Saturday Night Special got its name—but they're fun there, too, especially on the last midnight of December, when citizens take to the streets and fire them in the air. "It's like shooting out the old and shooting in the new year," one Detroit resident said before a recent celebration. "It's a tradition passed down to me from my father."

The tradition in which shooting passes down from father to son is even stronger in rural America, since the hunting culture is older and more deeply rooted there than in or around the cities. There is no general agreement on the age at which a boy should be given his first gun—only that it should be sometime before he reaches the age of sixteen. According to a brochure put out by the National Shooting Sports Foundation, "some youngsters are ready to start at 10, others at 14." But, the foundation advises, if your youngster is "conscientious and reliable," if you would "leave him alone in the house for two or three hours," or if you would "send him to the grocery store with a list and a $20 bill," then he's ready to be handed his first gun.

Among the many admirers of this tradition was the late Herman Kahn, of the Hudson Institute. In an essay defending it against attacks by "the American upper-middle class intellectual élite"—who are "ignorant and even bigoted" about "the family customs of American rural and lower income groups"—Kahn argued that the rural gun and hunting culture is "an excellent setting for raising children." And, recalling talks on the subject that he'd given to students at Berkeley, Brandeis, Columbia, Harvard, Princeton, and Yale, he wrote:

> I almost always started my discussion by asking some questions. One common question was, "How many of you have three guns of your own?" About 30 percent of the audience usually did. I then asked those who did not have guns at home why they thought the others owned so many weapons. Most of the nongun-owners were absolutely perplexed. They looked at the gun-owners in total bewilderment. What in the world would anybody be doing with three guns?

What the nongunners didn't realize, Kahn explained, was "that they lived in a hunting culture, that these were in effect rites of passage. . . . A boy who is given a .22 rifle becomes a young man almost overnight," and the "hunting culture gives young men a sense of meaningful identification with his pioneer ancestors, with traditional American history." Kahn went on to admonish the "upper-middle class urban Americans" and the "liberal press" for regarding the hunting culture as "perverse or perverted" and for treating "the gun as a kind of violent pornography." However, at a time in our history when hunting is no longer a necessary means of feeding the family it is perhaps hardly surprising that many Americans should regard as "perverse or perverted" the practice of killing animals, since they are now killed mainly as a pastime or as a hobby. As for the nongunners who view the weapon as "a kind of violent pornography," they're not alone. We have it on the authority of John Hinckley, Jr.—who, whatever the state of his mind may be, is neither liberal nor antigun —that "this gun gives me pornographic power."

To this argument Kahn could well have replied that it was the long gun he was discussing, not the handgun. But the liberal critics Kahn wrote about are, despite their aversion to hunting, less hostile toward the long gun than toward the handgun. It is chiefly the handgun that they associate with violent pornography, for it is the handgun that is most commonly used in confrontations where sexual power, virility, and machismo are supposed to be confirmed or confounded by the outcome. Examples abound—in personal disputes, in the movies, on television, and in the hardboiled school of detective fiction represented by best-selling authors like Mickey Spillane. According to a study by John G. Cawelti that appeared in the *Journal of Popular Culture* in 1969, "one main theme" of Spillane's writing is "violence as orgasm." And though, as in Spillane's fiction, women are often the victims or objects of gun machismo, a number of them have also used guns, since guns symbolize violent male power, which they may resent, admire, or envy. "There are women for whom the ideas of masculinity and fierceness are not to be disentangled from one another," Diana Trilling writes in her account of the Jean Harris murder trial. When the headmistress acquired the gun she used to kill the Scarsdale doctor, Trilling adds, she "became capable of assault. She was supplied with what she'd been deprived of by biology."

3

VISITORS TO THESE SHORES continue to be amazed by the freedoms of our gun culture. In 1982, Zhao Jinglun, a scholar from China, set out from Cambridge, Massachusetts, where he was staying, in search of "the real America." He was gathering material for a book to be called *The Americans: Their Culture and Institutions,* and people in Massachusetts had told him that the New Englanders he lived among were by no means typical Americans. One leg of Zhao's journey took him to Dallas and Houston, where he was shocked to see guns being sold in department stores. That sight, among others, led him to conclude immediately that Texans couldn't possibly be typical Americans, either. It's a conclusion he should have resisted: Texans are different from other Americans only in that they can buy their guns more easily and use them more freely than people in most other parts of the United States.

About twenty years before Zhao's visit, the writer John Bainbridge spent nine months in Texas preparing to write a book, *The Super-Americans,* about life and culture in that region of the country. Bainbridge found

that "gunplay . . . enlivens existence in Texas," that a
pistol could be bought as easily "as a fishing rod," and
that if a gun wasn't available in the house, a man could
"usually go next door and borrow one, as he would a
quart of milk."

For a number of years, until it was surpassed by
Miami, Houston was known as the murder capital of the
United States. Since 1982, however, that distinction has
been held by Odessa, a small but thriving oil town in
West Texas. That year, not nearly as many people were
murdered in Odessa as in Miami, Houston, St. Louis,
New York, or Dallas, but Odessa had the highest mur-
der rate. According to figures compiled by the National
Coalition to Ban Handguns, on the basis of the F.B.I.
Uniform Crime Reports for 1982, Odessa had 29.8 mur-
ders per 100,000 population, which pushed it past
Miami (with 29.7 per 100,000) to the head of the list. On
that list, three other Texas towns ranked among the top
ten—Houston (28.2), Longview-Marshall (21.6), and San
Antonio (18.5)—and Midland, Waco, and Dallas–Fort
Worth were in the top twenty.

In February of 1983 six men sat down to a friendly
game of Saturday-night poker in a quiet neighborhood
of Odessa. Early Sunday morning, while the game was
still in progress, a heavy loser excused himself from the
table and soon returned with a .38-caliber pistol. Claim-
ing that someone at the table was cheating, he pointed
his gun at each of the others in turn and ordered,
"Don't anybody move." Despite the order, one player
pulled a .45-caliber handgun, a second went for a pistol
of his own, and in the ensuing gunfight all three men

were hit. The player who had pulled the first gun staggered from the house, bleeding from his wounds. Down the street, he knocked on the door of a neighbor, and the neighbor, mistaking him for a burglar, shot him dead. Later, the two other men who had been shot at the poker table also died. Then there's Old Snake River, another small Texas town. According to one of its police officers, "All of the people are armed and they want everyone to know it. When you go to someone's house you have to knock on the door and step back and let them see you, because if you don't, you'll be looking down the barrel of a deer rifle." Nerves in Old Snake River are "strained," *Newsweek* reported in 1984, and it went on to tell this story of a young mother. Startled by a knock on her front door, she picked up a .38-caliber revolver, and challenged the caller: "You'd better open up and let her fly." The visitor, when he announced himself, turned out to be her family minister. "I'd hate to kill my own preacher," she said later.

The special feeling that Texans have for the gun—like the feeling for it in the country as a whole—springs from special circumstances in their history. The sovereignty of their state was won from Mexico partly by their superior use of the gun, and it's partly in recognition of that fact that the laws of Texas have made it so easy for citizens to acquire firearms. Mayor Bob Bryant, of Odessa, commenting in 1983 on the availability of handguns in Texas, added, "Maybe it goes back to the code of the West, people reacting by reaching for a gun." The sovereignty of the American nation was also won by the superior use of the gun, and while the laws of the United States have not, in general, been as lax as those of Texas, they, too—reflecting similar sentiments —have allowed gun enthusiasts far more freedom than have the laws of almost any other society.

Even before the gun helped to achieve the independence of Texas, it had been a popular "plaything" in parts of the South. In the antebellum era, more gun duels were fought in the Deep South than in almost all the rest of the nation. Settling ordinary differences or resolving questions of honor, the derringer and the duelling pistol snuffed out the lives of more "gentlemen" than did any other weapon. According to contemporary accounts cited by the historian John Hope Franklin, duels in Mississippi were as "plenty as blackberries"; in New Orleans "a jest or smart repartee" was "sufficient excuse for a challenge," and men there accepted the challenge to a duel "with the nonchalance of an invitation to a dinner or supper party." College students carried guns to their classrooms—as some high-school students do today. De Tocqueville noted when he came here that murders were common among Southerners, who preferred submitting their disputes to the adjudication of pistols rather than the courts of law.

The South wasn't the only duelling ground in America, of course. It was in the North—in Weehawken, New Jersey—that Aaron Burr shot down Alexander Hamilton, in what is probably the nation's most notorious duel. It was in Illinois that Dickens' Martin Chuzzlewit heard that in America a man could be shot down for speaking disparagingly of another man's favorite political ticket. And it was also in the North that Dickens read of legislators shooting down one another over insulting remarks made in the course of heated debate. One historian reports that the European press "occasionally criticized the United States as a barbarous country where such hostile encounters were to be expected among ruffians who lacked the refinements of an older, wiser civilization." But, of course, in some of these bloody engagements Europe wasn't always the paragon of refinement it claimed to be.

Nor did every American gentleman accept with nonchalance, or accept at all, the insane challenge to shoot it out at several paces. John Breckinridge's reply to one such challenge, in the late 1790s, has been called "the most rational document in the history of duelling." Breckinridge wrote to his challenger:

> Sir:
> I have two objections to this duel matter. The one is lest I should hurt you; the other, lest you should hurt me. I do not see any good it would do me to put a bullet through any part of your body. I could make no use of you when dead for any culinary purpose, as I could a rabbit or a turkey . . . for though your flesh might be delicate and tender, yet it wants that firmness and consistency which takes and retains salt. At any rate, it would not be fit for long sea voyages. You might make a good barbacue, it is true, being of the nature of a racoon or an opossum, but people are not in the habit of barbacuing anything human now. As to your hide, it is not worth taking off, being little better than that of a two-year old colt. As to myself, I do not much like to stand in the way of anything that is harmful. I am under

the apprehension you might hit me. That being the case, I think it most advisable to stay at a distance. If you want to try your pistols, take some object—a tree or a barn door—about my dimensions, and if you hit that, send me word. I shall then acknowledge that if I had been in the same place you would have killed me in a duel.

If it is true that people in New England aren't typical Americans, the territory they inhabit and the history they inherit did help originate the gun culture that has spread throughout the nation; for the states of New England and a number of other states of the Northeast were the cradles of shooting and gunmaking in America. The first generation of American marksmen sprang up chiefly in Massachusetts. The first in a series of American-made rifles was designed and built by the gunsmiths of Pennsylvania. The founding fathers of the nation's great gun industry—men like Samuel Colt, Eliphalet Remington, Oliver Winchester, Horace Smith, and Daniel Wesson—were born and raised in Connecticut and New York. And most of the better known gunmaking firms are still situated in the Northeast. Connecticut leads, with companies like F. Mossberg, Colt Firearms, Sturm & Ruger, Charter Arms, Marlin Firearms, Remington Arms, and U.S. Repeating Arms (formerly Winchester). Massachusetts follows, with Dan Wesson Arms, Harrington & Richardson, and Smith & Wesson. New York has Sterling Arms, Maryland has Beretta U.S.A., and New Jersey and Pennsylvania have smaller firms of their own. So the Connecticut River Valley (which includes parts of Massachusetts) remains what it was from the early days of the nation's history, the gunmaking capital of America—"the center from which most of the achievements of the industry have sprung," as a Smith College study observed some years ago.

4

THE ORIGINS OF GUN USE in America are honorable. The country *was* born, as it is said, "with the rifle in its hand." It probably couldn't have been born—or, at least, born so inspiringly—without that weapon in its hand. In 1774, more than a century and a half after the first colonists arrived, an English visitor wrote home to report that there wasn't a man born in America who didn't understand the use of firearms—that "it is Almost the First thing they Purchase and take to all the New Settlements." Such men *had* to rely on firearms. They mightn't have been able to live without them. Especially in the backwoods, the long gun was the instrument that put meat on their tables and defended them against the attacks of hostile native tribes. To help feed and protect their families, boys learned to shoot by the age of twelve. Men carried guns almost everywhere they went—even to church—as a potential defense against surprise Indian attacks. Without their guns the settlers might not have survived to fight and win the battles that led to the birth of their nation.

The early, necessary reliance upon the gun lasted for some time, as the nation grew and expanded westward. But long after the weapon had ceased to be indispensable to domestic survival and nation-building, generations of Americans continued to embrace and glorify it as a living inheritance—as a permanent ingredient of the nation's style and culture. Its role in the social and political origins of the country has been used not only to justify its continued position in civilian affairs but also to excuse the extraordinary rate of civilian gun violence, for which America stands without a serious rival in the world. "Ever since the days when our frontiersmen won their way and settled our country with rifle and axe," writes Philip Whalen, who is an ex-soldier, "the former has been the symbol of real manhood, and so it must always be." Rifle shooting for sport and war, he continues, "has always been associated with redblooded men." And, by Whalen's test, America has surely excelled, in real manhood no less than in redblooded men.

The historian Frederick Jackson Turner hypothesized in the 1890s that the frontier experience accounted very largely for the distinctive traits of American character and behavior, and this now-famous thesis is widely accepted as an explanation for important facets of the nation's personality. Still, not all students of history concur with Turner. There are some who maintain that the formation of the American character owes a good deal more to cultural antecedents in Europe than to the rough and improvised life of the early frontier. And there are others who subscribe to

Turner only halfway. Richard Hofstadter, for instance, argues that "when the frontier and its ramifications are given their due, they fall far short of explaining the persistence of the American gun culture." He goes on to ask, "Why is the gun still so prevalent in a culture in which only about 4 percent of the country's workers now make their living from farming, a culture that for the last century and a half has had only a tiny fragment of its population actually in contact with a frontier, that, in fact, has not known a true frontier for three generations?" Whatever the answer may be, part of it must lie in what historical sentiment, the written word, motion pictures, television, and the powerful gunmaking institutions have done to perpetuate the legend of American firearms in the nation's imagination.

The modern long gun has a distinctly American parentage, for it was devised to meet the special needs of pioneer life. For years after the first settlers arrived, the European-made musket was the predominant firearm in the country. But it was basically unsuitable to the demands of their experience in the wilderness. For purposes of hunting and self-defense, it was too heavy and too inaccurate. The settlers in Massachusetts and other parts of the East wanted a more efficient weapon. They wanted one with a longer barrel and a smaller bore, for greater power and accuracy; and they wanted a much lighter one, for hunting and traveling over longer distances. The gunsmiths near Lancaster, Pennsylvania, set about designing and building just such a weapon; and when it became available, in the 1720s, it was im-

mediately praised both for its efficiency and for its sleek
appearance. The Pennsylvania rifle, as some people
called it, was the most accurate and graceful-looking
rifle yet devised, and it became a marvelous aid to life
in the wilderness. Later on, used by frontier militia-
men, it performed so tellingly in the Revolutionary
War that the British spoke in terms of awe about the
"American rifle" that had made its way out of the backwoods.

As it happens, this firearm is celebrated in the annals
of the frontier not as the Pennsylvania rifle, but as the
Kentucky rifle; and for this "theft" of credit Pennsylvania has chiefly Daniel Boone to blame. Despite its
earlier deeds in New England and along other parts of
the Atlantic Coast, the rifle was not widely recognized
until it was carried by Boone in his explorations of Kentucky territory. Later, the pioneer families and adven-
turers who joined the westward journey took that
weapon along. But the rifle that had been used to mas-
ter the difficult conditions of life in the forests proved
unequal to the demands of survival on the plains. The
Kentucky was a single-shot rifle. After each firing, the
muzzle had to be stuffed with new ammunition, and
that was a perilous procedure on the plains. Out there,
a herd of buffalo could stampede while the weapon was
being reloaded, or a band of plains Indians could attack,
for they had learned to outwit the single-shot gun by
unleashing most of their deadly arrows immediately
after the pioneers had fired. Nor was the Kentucky
powerful enough to penetrate the thick and furry hides
of the buffalo, which, it seemed, almost every voyager

across the plains lusted to kill. Between the 1840s and the 1880s, partly to correct these shortcomings, a series of more powerful rifles—some single-shot and some repeating—replaced the Kentucky. Among them were the Henry, the Sharps, the Hawken, the Spencer, the Springfield, the Remington, and the Winchester. The Winchester was probably the most famous, and the best, of the lot. It killed more Indians, more white settlers (for it was used by the whites in range wars as well as by some Indian tribes, who, impressed by its powers, had added it to their arsenal), and more wild animals than any other long gun on the Western frontier. The Winchester has therefore been called the gun that won the West, though the distinction deserves to be shared with other plains rifles, like the Sharps and the Hawken, and such handguns as the Smith & Wesson and the Colt.

While helping to win the West, the new repeating rifles also helped to change the character of hunting in America. Hunting had been mainly a food-gathering enterprise in this country, in contrast to parts of Europe, where it was chiefly a pastime for the landed and the rich. But as the rifles became more powerful and sophisticated, and as gunmaking changed from a modest-sized craft to a mass industry, growing numbers of Americans began killing animals for sport or for profit—taking heads and antlers for trophies or procuring hides for the lucrative fur and leather markets of the East. All this was encouraged by the fact that America had an abundance and a variety of what hunters call big game, rivaling almost any other part of the world.

At one time no big game was more abundant than the buffalo. In the early 1800s, before the stronger and smarter rifles came along, over sixty million buffalo roamed the grasslands. Though the Indians had been killing buffalo for centuries—as a source of food and clothing—their numbers seemed inexhaustible. They began to seem less so after guns like the Sharps and the Winchester arrived; and by the 1880s the buffalo population had been virtually wiped out. There were no easier or more inviting targets than buffalo, grazing with a serene obliviousness of threat. They were large animals, and they had such poor eyesight that only their sense of smell alerted them to the presence of human predators—often too late, when the hunters were ready to open fire. Half a herd was sometimes slaughtered before the others fully realized their peril. Hunters had discovered that whenever one buffalo was killed many others in the herd—apparently mesmerized by the smell of its blood—milled around the victim for a time before they panicked and stampeded. Often, it was while the animals were circling a fallen comrade that the riflemen shot them down in droves. Carleton Putnam, a biographer of Theodore Roosevelt's, has described another method. "By carefully choosing his animals and killing successively those which attempted to break from the herd, the hunter could start them milling in a circle where they continued at his mercy until his ammunition was exhausted," Putnam writes. "Sometimes as many as a hundred buffalo would be killed by one man in this fashion within an hour." When the railroads came, travelers from the East enjoyed shooting down buffalo from the windows of moving trains. "I recall that the conductor was . . . apparently enjoying the fun and making no effort to stop it," one passenger reported. "He refused to stop the train and pick up the dead animals. 'What in hell do they amount to anyhow?' he inquired."

The buffalo was a casualty in the march of "progress" —the expansion of the nation, the rise of commercial and sport hunting as American vogues, and the developments in gun technology that helped to advance these activities. If the old Kentucky rifle—which had come to be called a "squirrel rifle"—hadn't been replaced on the plains by more sophisticated weaponry, the buffalo might have remained one of the great ornaments of the nation's wildlife. Even after losing much of their habitat, as prairies became farmland, they would surely have survived in larger numbers than they do today. But the buffalo hunter, in the words of one historian, "would have starved with a single-shot Kentucky, when his was a business of mass slaughter."

Theodore Roosevelt's favorite rifle, and Buffalo Bill's as well, was the Winchester. "By all odds the best weapon I ever had," Roosevelt called it. The testimonial couldn't have come from a more deeply respected source. Toward the end of the nineteenth century, when he shot deer, bear, big-horn sheep, and what were left of buffalo in the Dakotas, Roosevelt was probably the most widely admired outdoorsman and big-game hunter in the nation. The journalist Mark Sullivan called him "the outstanding, incomparable symbol of virility in his time." The attractiveness of that symbol

lasted well beyond his time, too; in fact, Roosevelt remains something of a patron saint in the memory of the
nation's outdoorsmen.

To people who have never fired a gun, and wouldn't
think of shooting an animal for sport, Roosevelt is a
puzzling example of that culture. On the one hand,
there was his apparent need to test his manliness and
his marksmanship against animals of the wild. On the
other hand, there was his gentleness, his refined, reflec-
tive, and poetic sensibility. David McCullough, another
of his biographers, writes: "His own brave and cheerful
front was what . . . the large proportion of his country-
men most loved him for. . . . Yet his favorite contemporary poet was Edwin Arlington Robinson, whose
themes were loneliness and the burden of personal
memory. The robust, quick-stepping, legendary 'T.R.'
was a great deal more pensive and introspective, he
dwelt more on the isolation and sadness inherent in
human life than most people ever realized." He truly
loved birds and animals, had a tender eye and ear for
their shapes and sounds. Yet he didn't hesitate to shoot
them down the first chance he got. One of the better
prose writers to have lived in the White House, he has
left this lovely description of the elk's mating call:

> It is a most singular and beautiful sound, and is very
> much the most musical cry uttered by any four-footed
> beast. When heard for the first time it is almost impossi-
> ble to believe that it is the call of an animal; it sounds far
> more as if made by an aeolian harp or some strange wind
> instrument. . . . Heard in the clear, frosty moonlight

from the depths of the rugged and forest-clad moun-
tains, the effect is most beautiful; for its charm is height-
ened by the wild and desolate surroundings. It has the
sustained, varied melody of some bird songs, with, of
course, a hundred-fold greater power. . . . There can be
no grander or more attractive chorus . . . under the
moonlight or in the early dawn. The pealing notes echo
through the dark valleys as if from silver bugles, and the
air is filled with the wild music.

Of a blacktail buck, "one of the most noble-looking of
all deer," he wrote, "Every movement is full of alert,
fiery life and grace, and he steps as lightly as though he
hardly trod the earth." And when a majestic-looking
bull elk stepped out into a clearing and stopped for a
moment to study the man who was waiting nearby with
a Winchester in his hands, Roosevelt—for a moment
before he pulled the trigger—couldn't help admiring
"his mighty antlers thrown in the air, as he held his
head aloft." The first shot struck just behind the elk's
shoulder; the second went through the lungs and
finished him off—just after the animal, suddenly realizing his danger, turned and staggered back toward the
shelter of the woods from which he had emerged. Approaching the elk to claim the prize of its mighty antlers, Roosevelt again made an admiring note of its
"massive and yet finely molded form." That finely
molded carcass was devoured overnight by a grizzly
bear, as Roosevelt discovered the next morning, when,
as it happened, he was out stalking that very grizzly. He
got him, too, as he wrote to tell his family back East: "I
found myself face to face with the great bear. . . .

Doubtless my face was pretty white, but the blue barrel
was as steady as a rock. . . . As you will see when I bring
home his skin, the bullet hole in his skull was as exactly
between his eyes as if I had measured the distance with
a carpenter's rule." Those two magnificent animals had
been shot partly as a proof of self and skill and partly
for what they would add to the collections of a trophy
room.

5

EVEN AFTER THE GREAT HERDS OF BUFFALO had almost disappeared, America remained rich in wildlife.
There was still an abundance of elk, moose, antelope,
and big-horn sheep; of pheasants, turkeys, ducks, geese,
grouse, and quail; of hares, squirrels, and rabbits. And
these, with the increasing supply of guns, offered opportunities for hunting that were as great as any in the
world. To the steadily growing number of sport hunters, the right to enjoy those American opportunities
was nearly as sacred as the right to life, liberty and—to
them it *was* the pursuit of happiness. "I have the oppor-
tunity to hunt as a free man in a free country, . . . and
not have to pay someone for taking such game," one
modern hunter has declared. "It's mine and yours; it's
wildlife that belongs to all of us, the people. . . . Americans are lucky to be able to have the freedom to hunt,
and the freedom to own and carry hunting arms."

There were close to twenty million hunters in America in 1980. Most were stalkers of big game, and what they bought and sold supported a thriving hunting economy. According to *Gun Week*, a hunting-and-firearms publication, hunters spent $8.5 billion on their sport that year, including $902 million for guns and rifles, $106 million for scope sights, $87 million for gun-magazine subscriptions, $95 million for handloading equipment, and $449 million for ammunition. A relative few of these hunters—though the numbers are substantial—shoot illegally and profit handsomely from what they take. In 1979, a rancher in Texas was booked for possessing over a million dollars' worth of furs from animals that had been shot out of season. Poachers make between $3,000 and $6,000 for a mounted elk head and as much as $15,000 for the hide and claws of a grizzly bear (now among the endangered species); though they get only from $5 to $6 a pound for fully grown elk antlers, newly grown ones bring as much as $120 a pound, since those, still covered by velvet, are highly prized in the Orient as the makings of a tea that is taken as an aphrodisiac. Every deer season, *Audubon* reported in 1979, the "bullet-dead" bodies of half a dozen elk are found in the woods around Gaylord, Michigan. If the eyeteeth were missing, that was a clear sign that the animals hadn't been shot by accident, for "a pair of teeth will fetch four hundred dollars on the watch chain of a member of the Benevolent and Protective Order of Elks."

The average hunter is not a poacher, however. He's a licensed gunman, and he kills not for money but mainly for sport; that is to say, he may eat the game he shoots or he may dismember it chiefly for the taking of trophies. For many a hunter, the pleasure lies in just being afield, tracking the animals, firing at them, and enjoying his feats of marksmanship. He belongs to a fraternity that takes to the woods each fall with all the excitement and camaraderie of ballplayers taking the field for the start of a big-league season. But, unlike the ballplayers, who perform before an informed intelligentsia of their sport, hunters engage in an activity whose pleasures are known and shared only by them. "You and I belong to a pretty special—and lucky—group!" the head of the North American Hunting Club said in addressing fellow-hunters at the start of the 1982 season. "The nonhunter can never understand it, because words alone won't do. . . . *Only* the hunter . . . has smelled, and will trade for few other smells, the aroma of egg-shell coffee, November morning air, guns and gunpowder, and a hunting cabin at night. . . . [Only he] has experienced the thrill that comes when, after many hours of waiting, you draw a bead on a buck."

Each year the town of Lander, in Wyoming, opens its season with what it calls the One-Shot Antelope Hunt. It's a competitive event, in which a rifleman must kill with his first shot any antelope he levels his sights on; and it annually attracts one-shot enthusiasts from all over the country. In 1982 it attracted no less an entrant than James Watt, who was then Secretary of the Interior. Watt is a native of Wyoming, and it was probably this fact, together with the assembly of shooters he had joined, that accounted for his words of greeting as he arrived in Lander from Washington. "It's good to be with real people," he said. He was once quoted as saying that there are mainly two kinds of people in the United States, liberals and Americans; and there could be little doubt concerning the identity of those he was now greeting as real people. Watt missed with his first shot, and took some good-natured ribbing from the fellows. But he hit with his next, killing an antelope from three hundred and fifty yards away. The Secretary then knelt over the dead animal, one hand gripping an antler, the other holding on to his powerful rifle, and grinned delightedly into a camera. Lewis Regenstein, who is the vice president of the Fund for Animals, wasn't at all amused when he heard of Watt's feat in Lander. "We don't think there's anything particularly sporting or virtuous about the nation's chief protector of wildlife gunning down a defenseless antelope," Regenstein said. It may be doubted, however, whether Watt, the real people of Lander, or the general hunting fraternity took serious note, or any note at all, of what Regenstein had to say.

There are rugged gunmen who argue that hunting provides an equal contest between them and the animals they stalk and shoot. One hunter says of deer, "They're smart, and I like to see if I can't be a little bit smarter." But what chance can the animals have against the intelligence and ingenuity of human beings? Their only natural advantages are speed and the ability to spot the sounds and scents of approaching danger—*if* they're lucky enough to be downwind.

Some of them do not readily run from human beings, and pay the price for their curiosity or their trust; the speediest of them are unable to outrun the man-made bullet; they have no idea when they're being set up for an ambush, when one organized group of hunters is driving them in the direction of another group, which is lying in wait to open fire on them; they can't know that the footprints they leave in the snow are the very marks by which hunters often track them to their doom; and they haven't yet found out what the dumbest hunter has always known—that they're easiest to kill when their mating season comes around, when, under the urge to procreate, they're least alert and responsive to the sounds and scents of approaching danger. If the animals are so "smart," it's a mystery how so many of them are destroyed.

The literature of hunting has been able to record atrocities like these recounted by Jack O'Connor, formerly gun editor of *Outdoor Life:*

> The animal wounded only in the abdominal cavity can, if pushed, travel a long way and is often very difficult to recover. On two occasions I have seen animals lose everything back of their diaphragms and yet travel. A big buck mule deer I shot dragged his stomach and intestines along the ground behind him for about 100 yards before he fell. He was dead when I got to him. A desert bighorn ram shot by a friend I was hunting with had his abdomen laid open by a .300 Savage bullet as he ran directly away from the hunter down a canyon. He ran out on a flat and when he jumped a barrel cactus the

protruding stomach caught in the thorns and was jerked out. The ram ran between a quarter and a half mile before he fell dead.

The class of hunter to which that writer evidently belongs includes a number of eager tyros who take to the woods mainly to inhale the air of virility that surrounds the sport of animal shooting. Some are such poor and indiscriminate gunmen—firing at anything that moves, wounding animals and leaving them to suffer lingering death in the bushes—that they are a distress to their more experienced and thoughtful brethren. Such gunmen, one skilled hunter has said, "get up in the morning and they get out of the car and they expect to have parties and learn something about the wilderness, and relive some of those old Zane Grey and Ernest Hemingway stories." They want to return home "and show their wives or their girlfriends what great hunters they are." But they "have no business" going out with guns, "except that it's become very big business for the arms people to get them up there." Phil Johnston, a director of the National Rifle Association, has written: "Those who know me, know that if I'm looking at birds, it's with the idea that sooner or later I'm going to shoot at 'em. To say that I love hunting and shooting is an understatement. More so, I love firearms."

In fairness to the enterprise, not all hunters are macho and insensitive about their "contests" with animals. Writing some years ago, about "the primitive desire to hunt with a gun," the outdoorsman George

Ingram appealed to "those who cannot experience that feeling." They should remember, he said, that "many of us venture forth, not as vicious and gore-crazed killers, but as human beings who carry with us such unsettling memories as that of a helpless rail bird cringing on the salt marshes." But one may still wonder why so sensitive a hunter, burdened by memories that are so poignant and unsettling, doesn't reflect upon the nature of his sport, reconsider its pleasures, and withdraw from it. However, poignant and unsettling memories *have* liberated a few sensitive hunters from that primitive desire. In 1962 one such hunter, Edmund Gilligan, wrote a moving account of an experience that caused him to put his gun away forever. He had traveled from the East out to Lander, Wyoming, where the one-shot riflemen assemble each fall; and he had killed an antelope, after the animal had paused not far away and considered him for an instant with a friendly play of its eyes. "I looked down at the dead beauty and vaguely regretted his destruction," the hunter wrote. For a period after he returned home, where the antelope's head had been mounted over his fireplace, he remained haunted by the memory of its friendly eyes. And there came a day when, looking once more at the ornament above his fireplace, he could bear the experience no longer. "Above the guns, I saw the head of my Wyoming antelope," he wrote. "His eyes . . . made of luminous glass . . . matched the eyes I had once seen gazing at me in such a friendly way. . . . The shock of regret struck me then harder than ever before. . . . I said to myself . . . *I will never again interfere in the lives of my fellow creatures.* I then took the guns down from the wall and put them into a closet, where they will always remain."

Many hunters, and even a number of nonhunting riflemen, defend the shooting of animals as an aid to wildlife preservation. They argue that grazing areas are limited, and that to save entire animal populations from starving to death it is necessary each year to "crop," or "harvest," the "surplus." In practical terms they may be right. But there's an antihunting movement in America, and its members are mostly amused by the hunter's claim that, in effect, he shoots animals not so much for his own pleasure as for the preservation of the animals themselves. And some of *their* methods of wildlife preservation have made them hated enemies of the hunters. The New York *Times* reported in 1983 that animal lovers armed only with tape players were strolling through the woods of New Jersey playing recorded music and causing the animals to disperse before the hunters arrived with their guns. This humane act got them in trouble not only with the hunters but with the law as well. In February of that year, a New Jersey legislator introduced a bill seeking to make it illegal for anyone to "interfere or attempt to interfere with the lawful hunting pursuit, killing or taking of an animal." The legislator was kind enough to say that his intentions were to protect both factions—the hunters (from harassment) and the animal lovers (from reprisals). He added, however, that if the music-players didn't cease and desist, then someone was "going to get hurt."

The implication couldn't have been clearer: someone was going to get "accidentally" shot by a hunter. The music-players weren't intimidated, however. "Wildlife belongs to everybody," one of them asserted. "We think it is audacious of hunters to say they can shoot animals but we cannot protect them."

Elsewhere in America there are several organizations—true or alleged advocates of wildlife survival—that take varied stands on the question of hunting. The Izaak Walton League sees hunting as "a valuable management tool." The American Humane Association doesn't object to "humane killing"—only to the "treatment of animals which causes pain and suffering." The Wildlife Legislative Fund defines its "primary purpose" as that of defeating "antihunting fanatics" and ensuring "the continuation of hunting throughout America." The National Audubon Society doesn't advocate hunting but doesn't oppose it, either—so long as it's "done ethically." The Outdoor Writers Association of America argues that "without a regular controlled harvest, many animal populations and the ranges they occupy would be impoverished." The National Wildlife Federation endorses "the hunter-sportsman who, during legal hunting seasons, crops surplus wildlife, which would otherwise be lost to a sometimes more cruel Mother Nature." And the National Rifle Association issues the reminder that "hunting is dominant among American traditions" and "has contributed substantially to our sound national character."

The plainly pro-animal groups mince no words on the issue. The Friends of Animals consider the shooting

of innocent wildlife to be "neither sport nor hunting."
In the view of the Humane Society of the United States,
sport and trophy hunting serves "no purpose beyond
the entertainment of the hunter." The Fund for Animals sees "nothing sporting about shooting defenseless
wild animals with a high-powered rifle." It adds: "Most
'game' animals are harmless to man and seldom have
anything near a fair chance to escape, much less fight
back. The only real risk to the hunter is the danger of
being shot by another 'sportsman.' So what is this 'contest' we keep hearing about between hunter and
prey?" That question comes from an organization that
is headed by Cleveland Amory, one of the nation's most
outspoken advocates of animal rights. Amory is also an
author, and in *Man Kind?*—a book that could serve as
a manifesto of the antihunting movement—he calls for
the release of "our wild animals from the bondage of
the arms manufacturers and the gun and ammo magazines."

Away from the hunting fields, there are millions of
other sports gunners—target shooters of all sorts, developing or sharpening their skills at gun clubs and gun
ranges throughout the nation. They aren't all just having fun, however. The "plinkers" may be playing, for
they seem to enjoy marksmanship for its own sake.
They enjoy shooting at objects like tin cans, balloons,
and playing cards, and their sport descends partly from
the famous Annie Oakley, one of the most accurate and
entertaining shooters in the history of the rifle. To some
other target shooters—who fire at likenesses and sil-

houettes of birds, animals, and people—the "fun" may be much more serious: *their* practice of marksmanship is either a substitute for hunting or a preparation for self-defense.

Of such shooters in New York, the *Times* gave this account in March of 1983:

> Last year, a record 9,268 applications were filed for handgun licenses in New York City, more than twice the number filed in 1979. . . .
>
> And for many who received the licenses, Saturday has become a day for practice.
>
> Gerald Preiser, president of the Federation of New York State Rifle and Pistol Clubs, said that when he founded the West Side Pistol and Firing Range 17 years ago, it "used to be very macho, very closed to women, very father and son, very blue collar." In the last few years, however, the membership has changed.
>
> "We're getting more and more sophisticated types these days," Mr. Preiser said. Photographers, artists, writers, lawyers, brokers, dentists, and doctors have boosted membership at the range to more than 1,000 people, a 20 percent increase over three years ago, he said. About 15 percent of the members are women. . . .
>
> Saturdays are the busiest days at the indoor range, in the basement of an office building at 20 West 20th Street. . . .
>
> Inside one of the bays, Arlene Maniscalco, who lives on the Lower East Side, aimed her .45 Colt automatic at a paper target of a man's silhouette 15 feet away, and fired. Each time she squeezed the trigger, the heavy pistol bucked in her hand. Within seconds, the center of the man's chest was blasted away.

She cranked in her target and poked her finger into the ragged hole her five bullets had made. "I don't want to become a statistic," she said. "If I thought my life was in danger, I'd kill. . . ."

"I believe in having guns," said Roman Chapa, who carries either a .45-caliber automatic or a .38-caliber Beretta in his hip holster at all times, whether at home in Rye, N.Y., or at one of the restaurants he owns. "And all my neighbors are arming up. But it's not talked about."

The scariest of the target shooters are the ones who call themselves "survivalists"—the potential inheritors of the earth. They are confident that the threat of a nuclear holocaust will indeed come to pass; they intend to survive it; and they are training themselves to win the civilian warfare they believe will ensue in the dust and rubble of Armageddon. They are setting up well-stocked retreats in the hills and woods of America, far from where they expect the big bombs will fall; and after the bombs have exploded, the survivalists will not hesitate to shoot any living remnants of the cities who invade their sanctuaries seeking food and shelter. Posters that they've already printed up make their intentions clear: WARNING!! TRESPASSERS WILL BE SHOT. SURVIVORS WILL BE SHOT AGAIN. Their movement has put out books with helpful titles like *Surviving Doomsday* and *Defending Your Retreat: A Manual for Combat After the Collapse*. A monthly magazine that caters to them, *Swat*, is directed at people "who take life seriously." And their favorite firearm is the Israeli-made Uzi submachine gun, advertised in *Swat* as "the best there is."

The target-shooting community is more than a little embarrassed by its "survivalist" components, for it likes to think of itself as a society of sporting gun lovers. Speaking in this vein, some time ago, the editor of one of America's most widely respected outdoors magazines, who also happens to have been raised around rifles and pistols, said to a visitor, "Target shooting is for me a great change of pace. I get a great deal of satisfaction from putting bullets in the center ring of a target. I can hit that ring twenty-seven times out of thirty. A Coke can makes a spectacular splash when you hit it from a distance of fifty yards or so. I may also shoot representations of a turkey or a ram or a pigeon. You must knock them over at a distance of one hundred yards. But I must say that there are definitely some dismaying aspects to the gun fraternity. For example, I think the survivalists, who think they're going to be around after the nuclear explosion, are giving the shooting fraternity a bad name. They go around with these paramilitary Uzi weapons, since these guns make them look so macho. They turn my stomach. There's no legitimate use for such guns in the civilian life of our country." He added, "Anyone who grew up in the Middle West, as I did, or *when* I did, grew up with guns. You started with rifles. You then graduated to handguns; and you went on from there to gun collecting. Good antique guns are sometimes better investments than blue-chip stocks. They can be very expensive—the

Colt Peacemaker, for example. There are guns from the Civil War period that will fetch thousands of dollars. Old guns like these give me a feeling of connection to American history itself. I find them to be things of absolute beauty. The Colt Peacemaker is an absolute dream. It's a joy to handle. And it's one of the most beautiful pieces of sculpture ever applied to a tool or instrument."

PART II

THE HANDGUN:
Romance and Tragedy

1

NO FIREARM has been more damaging to civilian life in America—has been used in more robberies, murders, and other physical assaults—than the handgun. Yet none seems to have been more highly romanticized as a symbol of the nation's bond with gunfire. Devotees of shooting may see nothing strange in that pair of facts. But Americans who are neither users nor lovers of guns undoubtedly do. It must seem a dreadful contradiction to them that a weapon devised chiefly for the purpose of killing human beings—and takes more than ten thousand civilian lives each year—should be the glamorous item of our culture that it is. It must astonish them to hear lethal handguns being praised for their "beauty" and "tasteful" design, or being called by such stylish names as the Pathfinder, the Minx, the Abilene, the Red Hawk, the Super Blackhawk, and the Diamondback. In his book *Great American Guns and Frontier Fighters*, Will Bryant writes of firearms as "household" and "matter-of-fact" items. And when the guns were very good, Bryant continues, "they began to acquire almost human traits. . . . Men said that a gun was 'noble' or that it was 'vicious' or 'sweet,' or gave it a name like Betsy." By itself a gun is "a cold machine, a thing of wood and metal," Carrol C. Holloway writes in *Texas Gun Lore*, but "clothed with the rich garments of dreams it cannot be cold." We learn from a review of Albert Goldman's *Elvis* that Presley "packed three guns in his later years," that he "kept one on the table while he ate," that he "thought nothing of running up an $85,000 gun bill," that he "thought nothing of drawing a gun on people who crossed him, or blasting away at a television set when a program annoyed him." Makers of the John Wayne commemorative Colt .45 call attention to its lovely ivory grip and its elegant packaging—"a deluxe hand-finished oak presentation case" with a "selective gold-plated plaque." They invite buyers to wrap their hands around the grip of a Colt and imagine themselves "right back through history" and feel "the same confidence" and "pride of possession" that the pioneers did when the Colt was "man's constant companion on the trail." More recently holders of the American Express credit card were offered the opportunity to obtain from the Franklin Mint re-created models of the .44-caliber Smith & Wesson revolver that Wyatt Earp used in the shootout at the O.K. Corral (in Tombstone, Arizona)—"the West's most celebrated gunfight." The offer goes on to state that the re-created version of Earp's gun "has an elegance that well bespeaks the style of a professional gambler and gunfighter."

In 1983 a bank in Findlay, Illinois, mixing the casual and the chic, offered depositors a pair of Colt handguns in lieu of interest. The offer brought in a deluge of new deposits, surpassing the "wildest dreams" of one bank executive. A reason for the deluge, another executive explained, was that there weren't many liberals in

Findlay; people there "still believe in God, guns, and guts as what made the U.S. what it is today." Believing in these things, the people of Findlay must also know that robberies with guns helped to make the United States what it is. But, because of the place that Findlay is, the bank probably has no fear that the guns it gave away could one day be turned against its own tellers. Findlay, residents say, is "a quiet bedroom"; the kids are "excellent"; no one "gets rowdy in Findlay"; and the town "is as dry as you can get, except on New Year's Eve." Besides, the movie house that used to be there has been torn down—the one social center in which kids might have been exposed to the epics of American gun robbery that Hollywood can present so effectively and seductively. Of course, there's nothing to prevent the kids from taking a ride into Decatur, the nearest big town, for a Saturday night at the movies. Findlay's wasn't the only, or even the first, bank to offer guns as interest on deposits. The Citizens First Bank of Ocala, Florida, did so in 1982, and Bob Mock, the bank's executive vice president, was quoted as saying that he got the idea from the Bank of Boulder, Colorado. When Mock's bank first advertised in local newspapers, "we got calls from the Ocala area" mainly, he said. But when the bank advertised in a national gun publication, "calls started coming in from all over the country."

A year before the bank in Findlay distributed its pistols, Southern California introduced what may be the highest form yet of handgun chic—"the ultimate status symbol," it has been called. This is the Bijan designer handgun, which is embossed in pure gold, and which can be equipped—on special request—with a set of golden bullets. It was produced by a designer named Bijan Pakzad, whose boutique, in Beverly Hills, has been known to stock $95,000 bedspreads and other conspicuously expensive consumer merchandise. At Bijan's boutique, one may also purchase a copy of his designer pistols, for as little as $10,000. Pakzad is also on record as making some rather proud statements about his handgun. Noting that "Gucci never did gold pistols," he has called them "a chic and elegant form of protection," a thing that everybody "who is rich and loves guns will want." He has said he designed "something so American" that even people who hated guns would want one, to touch and fondle, "because it's so pretty." He has expressed the view that every possession of "the discriminating man, including his means of security, ought to be of the highest quality and taste."

2

WHEN ORDINARY, or more serious, pistol lovers meet to discuss what they admire in the guns they use, names like Smith & Wesson, Charter Arms, Ivor Johnson, Browning, Ruger, and Beretta are almost sure to be mentioned—names of some of the major handgun manufacturers in the United States. But highly prized though these products may be, they aren't nearly as illustrious as the two handguns from which they all descend—the guns of Henry Deringer, Jr., and Samuel Colt. Deringer, a Pennsylvanian, sprang from a pre-Revolutionary gunmaking family. His father was one of the German immigrant gunsmiths who, in the 1720s, designed and built the venerable Kentucky rifle—the first of the distinctly American long guns. The younger Deringer made his own mark in the early 1850s, when he developed the pistol that bears his name (now spelled "derringer"). Light and palm-size—nothing like its contemporaries, the pepperbox and the longer duelling pistol—it was the tiniest handgun yet made. And because it was also accurate, and deadly at short range, it was widely adopted as an indoor gun, though mostly in towns and cities. In San Francisco, during the Gold Rush days of the 1850s, it was the favorite weapon of miners, gamblers, bankers, bartenders, brothel keepers, and women who risked entertaining strangers in their own boudoirs. Men carried it in waistbands, shirtsleeves, coat pockets, and the tops of high boots. Women wore it stashed under hats, corsets, garter belts, or in muffs or pocketbooks. It is no wonder that this clandestine weapon came to be known as the assassin's gun—especially after John Wilkes Booth, secretly armed with one, walked into Ford's Theater and shot down Abraham Lincoln. In short, the derringer was the Saturday Night Special of its time—the first of the easily concealable snub-nosed pistols that have become so prevalent and so murderous in the towns and cities of America.

But the derringer's early place in the development of civilian handgun violence has long been overshadowed by the Colt revolver—the famous six-shooter—which was invented a few years after the assassin's gun made its appearance. What made it a revolver, of course, was its revolving cylinder, containing chambers for separate bullets; it was one of the first pistols (after some of the older pepperboxes, which had revolving barrels rather than revolving cylinders) that could be fired several times in succession before it had to be reloaded. Unlike the derringer, Colt's gun wasn't ideal for indoor use. It wasn't concealable. It was long and heavy, sturdily built, powerful at long range, good for outdoor shooting. The inaugural model was a .34-caliber five-shooter, which, after undergoing a series of changes, led eventually to the .45 six-shooter of legend.

Sam Fields, a prominent modern advocate of handgun control, has written: "The modern handgun began its career of death and destruction . . . with the creation of the Colt .45 Peacemaker. . . . Such technology brought convenient ultimate violence within everyone's reach by supplying a dependable, easy-to-carry, ever-ready destructive device." Constructively and destructively—whether fired by the military, the police, or civilians—the Colt played a more dominant role in the affairs of nineteenth-century America than any other pistol. Its particular uses on the Western frontier bequeathed an appeal that has possessed the nation's imagination ever since. "Whatever the six-shooter may have to answer for," the historian Walter Prescott Webb has written, "it stands as the first mechanical adaptation made by the American people when they emerged from the timber and met a set of new needs in the open country of the Great Plains." Or, as an enthusiast of that weapon has put it, the Colt is "as much a part of our American heritage as the Constitution and Thanksgiving."

Samuel Colt, a Yankee from Connecticut, invented his revolver in the mid-1830s and built the first models in Paterson, New Jersey. And for the origins of the legend, Sam Colt and all the generations of Americans who came to revere his gun are deeply indebted to the state and people of Texas. There was no immediate demand for Colt's revolver when he invented it. The towns and cities of the nation had little or no use for so long and heavy and bulky a handgun. The nifty little derringer suited their indoor and short-range needs perfectly. The needs that the Colt revolver was ideally suited to meet existed at that time—in the 1830s and 1840s—mostly in the open spaces of the Southwest, and especially in Texas. Not only was the territory then struggling for independence from Mexico but, simultaneously, it had to defend its settlers against the attacks of hostile Apaches and Comanches. And the Texas Rangers—the chief military and police force of the territory—had found, much to their surprise, that the Indians were even more formidable adversaries than the proud Mexican soldiers. The Rangers, astride the finest horses in Texas, and armed with the best long guns then available—Kentucky-type single-shot rifles—were still outfought by the Indian warriors. Those Indians were superb cavalrymen—the most brilliant shooters (with arrows) from horseback in America—and they had no fear of the white men's firearm. They had learned from experience that the Texans, after firing, almost always had to dismount in order to reload—for those single-shot guns had to be reloaded through their muzzles, and it was nearly impossible to restuff a muzzle on horseback. Basing their strategy on this knowledge, the Apaches and Comanches would ride in only near enough to draw the first round of single-shot fire; then, while the dismounted Texans were reloading, the Indians would pour down en masse, strike quickly and devastatingly with their arrows, and swiftly retreat— before the surviving Texans were ready to start firing again. When the Rangers realized how the Indians were fighting them, they devised a counterstrategy. Instead of letting off their single-shot rifles all at once, they began staggering their fire, shooting in platoons. But this method was only slightly more effective, for the artful Indians now held back their main attacking forces, sending in only a few riders at a time, until it seemed clear that the enemy's ammunition was exhausted. They then bore down on the Texans and unleashed their fusillades of arrows. "It was a situation which called for great economy and precaution," one observer of the Texas struggle wrote. "It gave rise to such admonitions as 'Hold your fire,' 'Take steady aim,' 'Make every shot tell.' The marvelous marksmanship of that early day was due to the fact that the first shot was frequently the only shot."

What the Texans needed were multishot weapons that they could fire repeatedly from horseback and could easily reload without dismounting. They began getting their hands on some of these weapons around

1839, when a few of the revolvers that Sam Colt had built in Paterson found their way—by means that have never been explained—into the Rangers' camp. By whatever means the guns had arrived there, they were a godsend. During one of the first battles in which the Rangers rode with Colt handguns they killed more than half of an eighty-man Comanche force and put the rest to flight. Colt's gun had shifted the odds decisively in favor of the Texas settlers. And the Indians, retreating before such a weapon as they had never confronted in the past, called it a "spirit gun"—magical in its ability to deliver so many bullets in succession. Other tribes later used the same term when, on the Great Plains, they encountered such formidable repeating rifles as the Winchester. But it was the discovery and use by the Texas Rangers of Sam Colt's invention that guaranteed its role in future dramas of American life.

"Without your pistols," Captain Samuel Walker, of the Rangers, wrote to Colt, "we would not have had the confidence to undertake such daring adventures." In appreciation of the territory that had proved the worth of his handgun, and in recognition of the town in New Jersey where he had built it, Colt named the first model of his revolver the Texas Paterson. But, as a fighting man, Captain Walker had found limitations in that model that its designer could not have known about, and in his letter of praise to Colt he went on to suggest changes that he thought would make Colt's revolver an even more effective instrument of warfare. "With improvements," Walker wrote, "I think they can be rendered the most perfect weapons in the world for light mounted troops . . . the only efficient troops that can be placed upon our extensive Frontier to keep the various warlike tribes of Indians and marauding Mexicans in subjection. The people throughout Texas are anxious to procure your pistols and I doubt not you would find sale for a large number at this time." Whatever the changes were that Walker suggested, Colt incorporated them into an advanced design of his gun, and about a thousand of the new weapons were later delivered to the Rangers. They performed as well as Walker had imagined they would, helping the Rangers to complete their mastery of the Indians and of those Mexicans who had continued to raid the territory even after its independence.

With such a history of accomplishment, the Colt handgun became the favorite firearm of almost all gun users in Texas, and remained so even after Remington and Smith & Wesson had begun making *their* famous revolvers; for decades it continued to be more popular in that state than in any other part of the nation. Sam Colt continued to develop and improve his revolver through and after the Civil War years, and in 1872 he produced the most famous of all his guns—and probably the most famous handgun ever made. This was the .45-caliber Single Action Army six-shooter, otherwise known as the Peacemaker. It was used extensively and with great success by the armed forces of the United States; but it was chiefly in the hands of prairie pioneers and fighters that it became an American legend. And it was mainly Texans who introduced it into the life and affairs of the Great Plains.

Having been first carried into that territory by cow-boys, the Colt revolver soon became the chief weapon of outlaws, gunfighters, and lawmen—though they did, of course, use rifles as well. Mark Twain once said of a Smith & Wesson revolver he took West in 1861 that though it looked like a dangerous weapon, it "had only one fault—you couldn't hit anything with it." No one ever said that about the Colt .45. It was the peerless fighting small arm of its day. Well balanced and easy to handle, it pointed—someone said—as naturally and as accurately as a forefinger. With a Colt in his holster, no man on the frontier felt himself to be the inferior of a potential adversary. A frontier saying had it that God had created men of varying powers and abilities but Sam Colt had made them equal. The equality, however, may have continued only up to the point where men reached for their Colts, since some men were always faster than others at pulling and firing their "equalizers." For quite some time, those men were usually Texans; which isn't surprising, since so many of them may be said to have been born with Colt revolvers in their hands.

3

THE COLT'S JOURNEY from Texas across the plains and into the Western heartland of violence and lawlessness began with the spread of the cattle trade. By the end of the Civil War, there was a great hunger for beef in the large cities of the East. Texas was the nation's cattle domain, and the expanding railroads, on which its meat could be shipped to those who hungered for it, had some of their major Midwestern depots in Kansas. To feed the tables of the East, to enrich the coffers of the Southwestern cattle barons, and to make an arduous, modest living for themselves, cowboys began driving great herds of longhorns across the world of grasslands between Texas and Kansas. The journey often took months. And since it was perilous as well as long, the cowboys needed guns to protect themselves and their herds from Indians, rattlesnakes, and cow thieves. More often than rifles they carried the Colt revolver—first the five-shooter and later the six-shooting Peacemaker.

The railheads of Kansas where the cowboys delivered their droves of longhorns were rowdy little cowtowns like Wichita, Newton, Hays, Dodge City, Ellsworth, Caldwell, and—perhaps rowdiest of them all—Abilene. The towns were never more disorderly than when the cowboys came in, with their tons of beef-on-the-hoof. But cowboys weren't the only, or even the main, causes of this disorder, which often turned into gunfighting and murder. A town like Abilene, which one of its founders had named from the Bible, had its core of God-fearing citizens—legitimate businessmen of all kinds, and also sedate families from the East, who were transplanting themselves to the open and promising frontier. In his book *Small Town America* the journalist Richard Lingeman describes these pioneers in the cowtowns of the plains as "the correct Puritanical mix of piety and Yankee business sense." But there also came a horde of gamblers, swindlers, bank and train robbers, horse thieves, cow thieves, and professional gunfighters. And these elements, many armed with Colt handguns, stirred most dangerously to life when the cattle drives came in; when the banks were loaded with money; when cash was flowing from hand to hand; when the saloons and brothels and gambling dens were most lively; and when the cowboys—having just been paid, after their months on grassland trails—were out kicking up their heels and letting off steam.

Almost all cowboys were good shooters. They were Texans, after all, and the perils of their work demanded that they be skilled in the use of handguns. But few of them were violent men, or possessed the temperament of gunfighters. The trouble they caused in the cowtowns was mostly innocent trouble—the result of drunken celebration, much like the trouble that rollicking sophomores cause at the end of a spring semester. Cowboys did yell and whoop and shoot their guns off in the air, but most of them came close to committing acts of violence only when the lawmen of Kansas tried to put an end to their spree. Cowboys couldn't stand being arrested by such lawmen. Some of those cowhands hated to think that the money they made from herding cattle came chiefly from the East; others had fought with the Confederacy, and still resented the Yankees they lost to; and they weren't ready to submit easily to lawmen whom they saw as transplanted citizens of a region that had defeated them in the Civil War.

But in the rough towns of the frontier such cowboys

were the least of the lawmen's worries. The real problems were the hot- or cold-blooded bandits and gunfighters who terrorized the life of the plains. On the roster of infamous Western outlaws were Clay Allison, "swift as water" with his six-guns; John Wesley Hardin, said to have killed more than forty men in his lifetime; Billy the Kid, who in a relatively short career disposed of around twenty; Frank and Jesse James, the princes of bank and train robbing; the notorious Coleman, Clanton, Younger, and Dalton gangs; Belle Starr, "the queen of bandits"; Bill Longley, with about thirty murderous notches on his six-guns; and such other fearsome killers and marauders as Doc Holliday, Al Jennings, Butch Cassidy, and the Sundance Kid. These and many like them ruled the frontier underworld from the end of the Civil War to the beginning of the new century —and mostly, though not exclusively, with Colt .45s.

The lawmen whose unenviable duty it was to maintain a degree of order on the frontier—marshals and sheriffs, like Bat Masterson, Bill Tilghman, Tom Smith, Wild Bill Hickok, Ben Thompson, Pat Garrett, and Wyatt Earp—also relied heavily on their mastery of the big handgun. Masterson and Tilghman reigned, at different times, in Dodge City. Smith preceded Hickok as marshal of Abilene, where both men tried and failed to enforce mild gun-control ordinances. Garrett, a sheriff in New Mexico, ended the murderous career of Billy the Kid. Thompson once presided in Austin, Texas. Earp ran Wichita and, later, Tombstone, the scene of the gory gunfight at the O.K. Corral that has been celebrated so glamorously on the nation's movie screens.

"Talk about the rule of iron, we had it," the mayor of
Abilene said of Hickok's tenure there. Hickok was himself later gunned down during a card game. Not all
these men were angels before they became peace officers; no angel could have done the job they did. A number of them came out of dark and lawless pasts—had
been robbers and gamblers and killers before they
were hired to wear the lawman's badge. In fact, some
owed their lawful employment to town mayors who
had heard of their exploits and reputations as feared
gunmen. So in the frontier towns, as in much of urban
America at a later time, the handgun served both sides
of the law, worked both sides of the violent streets. In
those early days, as in our own, the handgun was the
main weapon of civilian murder and assault.

4

CIVILIAN GUN VIOLENCE did not begin with the invention of the Colt revolver, of course, or with the movement of cattle out of Texas. Charles Dickens, when he
came here first, had remarked upon the mania, the
"Institution," that shooting-down seemed to be in
America; and since Colt's gun wasn't yet in popular use,
the shootings that Dickens heard and read about must
have been done with derringers, pepperboxes, and
duelling pistols. Still, such shootings weren't then as
common in American life as they were later to become.

And when one looks at the modern widespread fascination with handguns, one can hardly help attributing much of it to the development of the mass-production gun industry (especially in the latter half of the nineteenth century) and what the popular media have done to glamorize the role of guns in the life of the frontier. Popular entertainment, by its heroic portrayals of gunfighters—whether they were respected lawmen or infamous killers and bandits like Billy the Kid and the James brothers—has made the handgun seem an even more attractive and desirable arbiter of civilian conflict than it already seemed. Of the Americans who have been so influenced—who are still enraptured by the gun legend of the Old West—a writer for the *Wall Street Journal* said some years ago, "For most, it's enough to get the experience vicariously—by watching TV or movie heroes reassuringly gun down the bad guys. But for some the lure of the legend is great enough to cause them to acquire Peacemakers of their own."

Even before the popular media began their work, well-bred Easterners who visited the frontier had been returning home with exciting reports of the new style of life they saw out there and the new kind of heroic American that the rough Western experience was breeding. They misjudged much of what they saw, however. The historian Walter Prescott Webb has written: "The West appeared romantic to those not of it— to the Easterner who saw the outward aspects of a strange life, without understanding its meaning and deeper significance." Whatever the Easterner didn't understand, Webb went on, "was romantic, spectacular." He didn't "ride horses," didn't "wear a six-shooter," didn't "herd cattle or wear boots or red handkerchiefs or spurs," and couldn't "quite see that a normal person could do such things." So when the Easterner saw the man of the West, he "was at once impressed with the feeling that he had found something new in human beings."

It was Easterners—of whatever breeding or background—who began writing the cheap escapist fiction of Western life that quickly became a staple of popular reading. And what some of those stories made of the cowboy—presenting him, for example, as an outlaw and a gunman—bore little resemblance to the truth. Such stories probably took their evidence from the fact that almost all cowboys were Texans, and that Texans were almost always involved in frontier gunplay. But not all Texans were cowboys; and cowboys were seldom killers or gunfighters. They were chiefly hardworking men, plying one of the more dirty and unromantic trades on the frontier. Henry Chrisman, an authority on the Old West, has explained that real cowboys were "men who lived with their herds and knew no other life"; they "smelled of cow and horse dung, and seldom bathed"; they "wore beards that easily became nests of lice, fleas, or other vermin"; and their underclothes were changed periodically, spring and winter, and were washed when occasion permitted." One would find "nothing romantic or glamorous in the appearance of an old-time genuine cowboy," Chrisman adds. The old-time genuine cowboy, one gathers, would be amused beyond words were he to return and see what stories and movies have made of him.

It was also Easterners who invented the Western. *The Great Train Robbery* (1903), one of the earliest of such movies, was shot in the East, in the New Jersey countryside; and Edwin S. Porter, who wrote and directed it, was born and raised in Pennsylvania. This genre of film entertainment was as American as baseball, apple pie, and the stickup. Its appeal flowed from fast action, swift horses, the landscapes and horizons of the West (real or ersatz), the clash of good and evil, and the constant belching of gunfire. If all the gunmen weren't moral heroes, they were all heroes of a kind— exemplars of a distinctive American style. A bad guy was not exempt from capturing the affection of a movie audience if he had qualities of fast and exciting gunmanship. No man in a Western picture was worth much, was feared or respected, unless he carried a gun and knew how to use it. His mastery of that weapon— and, through it, of his adversary—was a sign of the manliness, the physical heroism, that audiences took to be typically and admirably American. That was probably why unarmed idealists and moralists—teachers, preachers, wandering intellectuals, and other men of Eastern "culture"—sometimes looked faintly ridiculous in a Western movie.

Westerns were not, to be sure, documentaries. They were an art form—an art form that translated reality, or what it took to have been reality, into entertainment. But even such a form may be expected to mirror shapes of the truth. And the Westerns' view of reality was often so erroneous that what they mirrored didn't so much translate as falsify and romanticize the truth about the past. Audiences, since many among them hadn't read the history books, could hardly be blamed for accepting the glint and glamour of movie-style gunfighting as a representation of what the real thing had been. It is hardly their fault that a pathological killer like Billy the Kid lives on in the national imagination as, in the words of a modern commentator, "a demigod of the Western myth." Law-abiding Americans of the Old West saw nothing remotely godly about Billy. To them, he was one of the more hideous by-products of the heroic and arduous pioneer struggle to build and extend the nation westward. Even the genuinely heroic peace officers took a less romantic view of shootouts than the Western movies later did. The peace officers were tough and brave men, but they feared for their lives, and many of them disliked having to kill. They knew better than almost anyone else how necessary but also how terrible a weapon the gun was. In the early years of this century, after Bat Masterson had retired from law enforcement on the frontier and was living in New York, President Theodore Roosevelt offered to reassign him to Indian territory as a marshal. Masterson begged to decline. "It wouldn't do," he told the President. "The man of my peculiar reputation couldn't hold such a place without trouble. . . . I'd have some drunken boy to kill once a year. Some kid who was born after I took my guns off would get drunk and look me over. . . . In the end, he'd crawl round to a gunplay and I'd have to send him over the jump. . . . My record would prove a never-failing bait to the dime-novel–reading youngsters, locoed to distinguish themselves and make a fire-eating reputation, and I'd have to bump 'em off. So, Mr. President, with all thanks to you, I believe I won't take the place. I've finally got out of that zone of fire and I hope never to go back to it."

Not unlike the shooting described in the dime novels, Western movie gunplay took an intense and, in some cases, a lasting hold on the fancies of the young—even many who didn't grow up to adopt the handgun as an analogue of baseball and apple pie. At the age of forty-six, Sherwood Anderson described the effect that Wild West movies still had on his imagination:

> Even today I cannot go into a movie theater and see there some national hero as, say, Bill Hart, without wishing myself such another. . . . Now he springs lightly off a horse and goes toward the door of a lonely cabin. We in the theater know that within the cabin are some ten desperate men all heavily armed. . . . Bill stops at the door of the cabin and looks at his guns, and we in the audience know well enough that in a few minutes now he will go inside and just shoot all those fellows in there to death, fairly make sieves of them. . . .
>
> All these things we know, but we love our Bill and can hardly wait until the shooting begins. As for myself, I never see such a performance but that I later go out of the theater and, when I get off into a quiet street alone, I become just such another. Looking about to see that I am unobserved, I jerk two imaginary guns out of a hip pocket and draw a quick bead on some nearby tree. . . . As I sat in the movie house it was evident that Bill Hart was being loved by all the men and women and children

sitting about, and I also want to be loved—to be a little dreaded, and feared, too, perhaps. "Ah! There goes Sherwood Anderson! Treat him with respect. He is a bad man when around."

5

IN 1922, when Anderson wrote those recollections, the Western movie was, at most, a quarter century old— one of the very first pictures of that kind being *Cripple Creek Barroom,* which was made in the late 1890s. By 1922, Anderson, who was born in 1876, must have seen not only William S. Hart but also other such early Western stars as Bronco Bill Anderson, Tom Mix, and Hoot Gibson. He couldn't yet have seen Roy Rogers, Bill Elliot, Gene Autry, and William Boyd, who helped make the Western even more popular. Nor could he have seen the modern gun flicks that brought the genre to the height of its appeal—classics like *Stagecoach* (1939), *My Darling Clementine* (1946), *Red River* (1948), *The Gunfighter* (1950), *High Noon* (1952), *Shane* (1953), *Gunfight at the O.K. Corral* (1957), *Man of the West* (1958), and *Lonely Are the Brave* (1962). It was probably after World War II that the Western truly came of age —at least, in the sense that some of the best-made and most memorable movies of that genre appeared after the war. That age has faded now, but while it lasted it inspired perhaps the most prolific production of Westerns that the nation has seen. *Life* reported in 1956 that Americn films had gone "gun happy," that Hollywood had turned out just during that year eight movies with "gun" in their titles, and that actors were "busy learning to shoot and be shot." The new films were milking the gun craze that the earlier ones had helped to foster, and the gun craze was sustaining itself on the nourishment of the new films.

By then, Westerns were surely not the only movies with guns and shooting in them. "The early twenties," the film historian Carlos Clarens writes, "were closer to the Wild West than Watergate." He was thinking of the spate of crime pictures mirroring aspects of the Roaring Twenties that Hollywood began releasing in the early 1930s. Like the Westerns, they memorialized the status of guns and gunmen in the nation's social life—only *their* weapons included submachine guns, and *their* gunmen were modeled on the crooks and gangsters of the Prohibition era. In the 1920s, the big cities of the East and Midwest, plagued as they were by murderous gunfire, became a second "West," a second "frontier" —a transformation that was influenced to a degree, no doubt, by the national romance with gunslinging that Western movies and dime novels had helped to promulgate. Chicago "was afflicted with such an epidemic of killings as no civilized modern city had ever seen," Frederick Lewis Allen wrote in *Only Yesterday*, his excellent portrait of the 1920s. New York could not have been far behind Chicago. And many of the new gangster movies were set in these two glittering towns—the

Tombstone and Dodge City, perhaps, of urban America. However heinous the Prohibition hoodlums and gunmen were in flesh and blood, there was often something engaging about them when their life and deeds were flashed on the screen—especially when they were portrayed by such icons of the cinema culture as James Cagney, Humphrey Bogart, George Raft, Paul Muni, and Edward G. Robinson. The gangster had become yet another star boy of the movie houses—another that made gunplay and gun murder an exciting form of entertainment. When they left the movies, grown men imitated the accents and struck the poses of stars like Bogart and Robinson and Cagney.

It would be foolish to claim that because of the orgies of gun murder they witnessed on the screen moviegoers found killing itself to be attractive, but not so foolish to say that many did find the gun to be attractive. And gun-killing was such a commonplace of those movies, so casual, even gratuitous, an incident, that it cannot have been difficult for viewers to become desensitized to the true and awful nature of the act. Unless it was the blowing of a kiss, nothing looked easier on the screen than pulling a trigger that released an invisible and impersonal bullet. No human contact was necessary. There wasn't a neater or purer gesture of violent murder. There wasn't a more abstract instrument of killing than the gun. It isn't surprising that American speech, borrowing freely from the language of gun movies and the crime culture, has so easily adopted bloodless euphemisms for "murder" like "rub out," "ice," "off," "blow away," and "terminate."

When television began its own influential career, in the early 1950s, it took up not only with the new tough-guy crime flick but also with that beloved old swaggerer the Western. According to a 1982 issue of *Guns & Ammo* magazine: "In the early 1950s, with television gaining a foothold in more than half of the American homes . . . the cowboy once again rode into America's imagination and in his holster he carried, as did his real-life counterpart in the last century, the . . . Colt six-gun. In the hands of the newfound heroes, the Colt was once again proving itself. Roy Rogers, Gene Autry, and John Wayne became as closely identified with the Colt as did Masterson, Earp, and Garrett." And some of the most absorbing series on television were to be shows like *Gunsmoke, Have Gun Will Travel, The Rifleman,* and *Wanted Dead or Alive.* "At every nightfall, twenty to thirty million American homes rock with the sound of sudden gunfire," an article in the *Nation* said in 1959. "The gunmen are merely TV actors acting as if . . . they were living west of the Mississippi in the brief period following the year 1870." Certain consequences were to be expected, and they occurred. According to a *Life* article ("Bang! U.S. Boys Bite the Dust"), "small fry" were to be seen "crumpling from imaginary bullets, then rising again to whip gun from holster and fill the air with the bark of make-believe shots." Credit for the dramas of gunfire that the small fry were reenacting didn't belong to movies and television alone. It was to be shared by the nation's toymakers, who estimated in 1956 that their sales of toy guns for that year would exceed thirty million. And by the early 1960s—before a temporary sag, caused by uneasiness over the war in Vietnam—toy-gun sales amounted to $100 million a year.

If gun movies and television shows had saturated the imagination of children—as they had saturated the imagination of their elders—it doesn't mean that the children always understood the violent meaning of their behavior when they reenacted the shootouts they had witnessed on the screen. Pauline Kael has written of "the naïveté of our own childhood, when we had innocently believed in the faultless protector-heroes." And Robert Warshow, an earlier judge of the film culture, issued this bit of advice: "Watch a child with his toy guns and you will see: what most interests him is not (as we so much fear) the fantasy of hurting others, but to work out how a man might look when he shoots or is shot. A hero is one who looks like a hero." Warshow went on to say, however, that the man wearing a gun "lives in a world of violence," and that his "image" or "style" is one that "expresses itself most clearly in violence." Therefore, the hero that a child would like to resemble must be such a man. And, if so, violence is what clearly defines the heroism that the child wishes to emulate.

A report released in 1982 by the National Institute of Mental Health concludes that "violence on television does lead to aggressive behavior by children and teenagers who watch the programs." In an article ("Mass Media Violence: Effect on Children") published in a 1969 issue of the Stanford Medical School journal, the social scientist Alberta Engvall Siegel cites studies showing that "young children imitate with fidelity the aggressive behavior they observe adults perform," whether the observation is in real life or on a screen. Among the studies she cites is one conducted by the *Christian Science Monitor,* during the first six weeks after the murder of Robert Kennedy. The *Monitor* found that the most violent evening hours on television were between seven-thirty and nine o'clock, when an estimated 26.9 million children, between the ages of two and seventeen, were watching. During those hours the study also found there was a murder or a killing every thirty-one minutes. In 1981, Representative Ron Mottl told the House Subcommittee on Telecommunications, which was holding hearings on "The Social/ Behavioral Effects of Violence on Television," that "the average high school graduate has been exposed to 18,000 television murders." The subcommittee also heard testimony from a number of other witnesses. Dr. George Gerbner, of the University of Pennsylvania's School of Communications, said, "Humans threaten to hurt or kill and actually do so—which is basically our definition of violence—mostly to scare, to terrorize, or otherwise impose their will upon others. Symbolic violence carries the same message. It is a show of force. It is a demonstration of who can get away with what and against whom. Basically our opinion is that those are the lessons it teaches. . . . And indeed our study shows that many of these messages are conveyed to the viewers. . . . Television has brought about the virtual immersion in violence into which our children are born." Dr. Thomas Radecki, a psychiatrist affiliated with the National Coalition on Television Violence, testified, "I can comfortably estimate that 25 to 50 percent of the violence in our society is coming from the culture of violence being taught by our entertainment media, most strongly by the television and movie industries."

The New York *Times* carried this report in April of 1983:

> "There can no longer be any doubt," said Dr. Leonard D. Eron, of the University of Illinois at Chicago, "that heavy exposure to televised violence is one of the causes of aggressive behavior, crime, and violence in society." Television violence, Dr. Eron said, "affects youngsters of all ages, of both genders, at all socio-economic levels, and all levels of intelligence. . . ."
>
> According to a study made by Dr. [Linda S.] Lichter and her husband, S. Robert Lichter, 250 criminals turned up in 263 prime-time programs in [the] 1980–81 season. They committed, she said, 417 crimes, or an average of 1.7 per show. . . .
>
> On the small screen, she said . . . murder is 200 times more prevalent than it is in reality, and television crime in general is 12 times more violent than crime in real life. . . .
>
> Though John W. Hinckley, Jr., may have failed to kill President Reagan when he shot him in 1981, Mr. [Daniel] Schorr [the news commentator] said, he successfully manipulated "a medium that celebrates violence" and made himself into "a media celebrity." He cited Mr. Hinckley's first question to his Secret Service interrogator: "Is it on television?"

No doubt all such testimony could be and has been contradicted by many other witnesses.

In any case, why is it that our film shows are so full of gun violence? Max Lerner's answer, in his now-classic work *America as a Civilization,* may be instructive: "The American conquers as a man of action, he puts his fate in action, and he expects action in his movies." It may be, he adds, that "movies reflect the strain of interior violence and tension in the culture." Warshow, probably an even more astute interpreter of the phenomenon, makes a similar point when he states of Westerns that they "offer a serious orientation to the problem of violence as can be found almost nowhere else in our culture."

PART III

RIGHTS IN CONFLICT

1

IT HAS BEEN CLEAR for generations now that Americans are more prone to violent confrontations with one another than are people in any other developed society, and that the issue is often settled by someone's pulling the trigger of a handgun. Yet the death toll from those confrontations has continued to rise. Between November of 1963 (when President Kennedy was assassinated) and November of 1982 (after President Reagan barely escaped assassination in 1981), nearly half a million civilians were killed with guns—by murder, accident, or suicide—and almost five million more were robbed, wounded, or raped at gunpoint. Between 1963 and 1973, while the war in Vietnam was taking 46,121 American lives, guns here in America were killing 84,644 civilians. Statistics for the first few years of the 1980s are just as appalling. It has been estimated that between fifty million and sixty million handguns were owned by civilians, and, according to the United States Bureau of Alcohol, Tobacco, and Firearms, two million new ones were being bought every year. The F.B.I. Crime Reports reveal that in 1981 there was one violent crime in America every twenty-four seconds, one aggravated assault every forty-nine seconds, and one murder every twenty-three minutes—the majority of such offenses being committed with firearms. Of the murders committed in 1981, which totaled 22,516, 50 percent were committed with handguns, 8 percent with shotguns, and 5 percent with rifles; knives and other cutting instruments accounted for 19 percent, and "personal" weapons—hands, fists, and feet—for 6 percent. The remaining 12 percent were committed by a miscellany of other means. In 1983 a study published in the *New England Journal of Medicine* reported that pistols accounted for 83 percent of all firearms used in suicide. "It is conceivable," the study said, "that the rise in the suicide rate might be controlled by restricting the sale of handguns."

Some of these figures may or may not be striking to leaders of the nation's pro-gun movement, who maintain strongly the view that guns don't kill people— people do. If they're right, in any but the most literal and simplistic sense, then why were only 6 percent of all the murders in 1981 committed with the "personal" weapons of hands, fists, and feet, while 63 percent were committed with guns? The statistics suggest that guns, by their very nature, make it easier for people to kill than other weapons do. It would appear, then, that if there weren't so many guns at large, and if they weren't so easily available, there would be much fewer murders than there are. D. H. Lawrence once asserted that the American soul "is hard, isolate, stoic, and a killer." As long as the leaders of the pro-gun movement maintain that people are killed by people, and not by guns, then —faced with the fact that there are more murders in the United States every year than in any other advanced society in the world—they can scarcely dis-

agree with Lawrence's judgment that we are a nation
of killers. Other people might prefer to say that there
are just too many guns in America, that America is
much too fond of guns, and that Americans find it far
too easy to acquire and own guns.

Two psychiatrists wrote in 1969: "If the United States
had the same gun homicide rate as Japan, our 1966 gun
death toll would have been 32 instead of 6,855; if our
suicide rate by gun were the same, only 196 persons
would have killed themselves with a gun instead of
10,407. Our homicide-by-gun rate is 35 times that of
Germany, Denmark, England, and seven times that
of Canada and France." In 1980 a London newspaper
called John Lennon's murder a "peculiarly American"
death. And according to another paper from that city,
the freedom to carry guns "has brought forth mon-
sters" in the United States. That year there were eight
handgun murders in England and 11,522 in the United
States.

Millions of the handguns now in America were acquired for self-protection—which isn't hard to understand, for the crime rate is alarmingly high and the fear
of crime has never been greater than it has been in
recent years. "I've worked too hard for what I've got to
let anybody take it away from me," one homeowner
said in 1981, soon after going out and buying himself a
handgun. "I already went through the normal proce-
dures of barring myself in my own house. I have a dog,
I have all the preliminaries. I even thought of tear gas.
And there's no point in my moving somewhere else, it's
everywhere. And the police can't always be where

they're needed. So I bought a gun." And many home-owners like him have had reason to be glad that they acquired guns to protect themselves and their families. Yet a terrible irony of this justifiable precaution is that guns bought for family and self-protection end up doing far more harm to the owners, their loved ones, and their personal acquaintances than they do to intruders. As Mark Twain once wrote, there's no more dangerous weapon in the house than an "unloaded" gun. According to the F.B.I., 55 percent of the murders committed in 1981 were "by relatives or persons acquainted with the victims." And 17 percent of those murders were within domestic relationships. In addition to such killings, a considerable number of deaths and injuries were caused by suicides and gun accidents.

In the Bronx, a four-year-old girl shoots and seriously wounds her two-year-old brother; she had believed the gun to be a toy. In New York's Westchester County, an actress shoots herself in the abdomen while trying to unload a gun. In Wyoming, a man returning home is met and fatally cut down by a hail of bullets; the assailants are his son and daughter, aged sixteen and seventeen. When, despondent over the coming divorce of his parents, a thirteen-year-old boy in Georgia puts a gun to his head, the mother begs him to take her life instead; he obliges, putting a bullet through her skull. During an argument that breaks out at a wedding party in Colorado, the mother of the bride fires a gun at her husband, misses him, and hits and kills her new son-in-law. In Brooklyn, a sleeping three-year-old boy is killed by a bullet his father had aimed at his mother. Those aren't just incidents that *can* happen when there's a gun in the house. They and hundreds of others actually occurred in 1982 and 1983. There had also been this incident, in 1981, reported by the New York *Times:*

> Mr. Fredette had just come in from feeding the animals. . . . His middle daughter . . . who did not like guns, was ironing a pair of jeans . . . preparing to go out with her friend Mary James. . . . Miss James said something to the effect that she didn't like guns. . . . Mr. Fredette stopped directly before her . . . unholstered the gun, unchambered it, emptied a load of shells into his left hand, closed the hand on five—which he apparently thought were six—shells, snapped the chamber shut, and pointed the six-inch barrel at the juncture of his nose and forehead. . . . He looked at Miss James with his crisp blue eyes. "Do you think I would do this if it were loaded?" he asked. As the two young women watched, he pulled the trigger twice. The gun made an oiled clicking sound. He pulled it a third time, and the firing pin struck the waiting sixth shell. This bullet entered Mr. Fredette's head but did not exit. He died instantly.

Gun owners aren't swayed by any such evidence, however. After the *Times* said in a 1982 editorial that "a gun in the home is virtually useless as a deterrent of crime" and that "more than 90 percent of break-ins occur while residents are away from home," a gun-owning reader, in a letter to the editor, denounced the paper's comments as "patronizing and elitist." People "are not concerned about accidents by family members," the letter said. The "number one issue is terror and fear of vicious criminal attacks by unknown, depraved criminals." There's truth on both sides of that exchange, and it indicates why for some time to come there may be an impasse in the gun debate. On the side of the letter writer, there is indeed the terrible rate of crime and the justifiable fear of it. On the side of the *Times,* there are the statistics showing the counterproductive presence of guns in the home: that they're far more damaging to family members than to the criminals they're meant to dissuade; that burglars don't, as a rule, break and enter when they have reason to believe that someone's at home; that when they do break into an armed and unoccupied home the loot, along with cash, that they find most irresistible is a handgun; and that more than two hundred thousand handguns are stolen from private homes every year—swelling the considerable arsenal already in the streets.

2

THAT ARSENAL is made up chiefly of snub-nosed handguns—or snubbies, as they're called. The snubbies are even more dangerous than bigger handguns for the obvious reason that they are so easily concealable. With their two- and three-inch barrels, nicely palm-size, they nestle snugly in a coat pocket without showing the slightest bulge. One cannot tell when one is in their presence. But they're usually up to no good, except when they're serving the defensive needs of law-abid-

ing citizens. Even then, they're strictly for killing or
wounding people. They may look like toys—they're so
cute and petite—but, especially at short range, they
pack a devastating wallop. The reporter Joseph Albright says of them, "One flick of the trigger and out
barks one-third of an ounce of lead at 735 miles per
hour, shaped to plow a mushroom cavity in someone's
gut." Most of these weapons are of two kinds. The better and more expensive kind is made here in America
and costs from $100 to $400. It's highly prized among
killers and robbers, but it's hard to come by in the
streets, for its price puts it beyond the means of the
average criminal. But since even the average criminal
knows a fine "piece" when he sees one, he often goes
directly for it when he breaks into a gun store or a
middle-class home—where it probably wasn't called a
snubby but, more respectably, a minigun, a midget
gun, a lady's gun, or a baby pistol. It is mostly when a
concealable handgun, expensive or cheap, falls into the
hands of hoodlums that it is referred to as a snubby. And
it is the cheaper kind—assembled here with parts imported from Germany, and costing $50 or less—that is
most prevalent in the streets. Because it costs so little
and is widely used in certain urban black neighborhoods—where it has been known to take more lives
than illness and auto accidents combined—the cheap
snubby is also called a ghetto gun. It is even more commonly described as the Saturday Night Special, a term
that Robert Sherrill explains in his book of that title: "In
the late 1950's and early 1960's, when mischievous residents of Detroit could not get their hands on guns in

their hometown, they would simply hop in their cars and tool down to Toledo, Ohio, less than an hour away, where guns were sold in candy stores, flower shops, filling stations, shoeshine stands, anywhere at all. Since a great many of those purchases were made to satisfy the passions of Saturday night, Detroit lawmen began to refer to the weapons as Saturday Night Specials." By that name, Sherrill goes on to say, "the language of America was enriched." Indeed it was. So much so that inner-city blacks, if they were once the principal buyers and users of Saturday Night Specials, have been joined over the past decade or so by the other races and colors of America. "We used to find guns primarily in poor neighborhoods," a New York City policeman said in 1975. "Now it's getting into the better neighborhoods." John Hinckley, son of a wealthy white family, used a Saturday Night Special in his attempt to kill President Reagan. Mark Chapman used one to murder John Lennon. And Arthur Bremer used one to cripple George Wallace. In several Western and Southern states, almost anyone may enter a gun store and leave with a snubby. In Texas, where Hinckley got his, buying a handgun takes only a little more time than buying a pair of boots or a six-pack of beer: one has only to prove that one is twenty-one or over, produce a driver's license, and assure the gun dealer that one is not a drug addict or a convicted felon. The pawnbroker who sold Hinckley his snubby later reported that the young man met every requirement for buying a firearm in Texas. "People are going to blame us for selling the gun that shot the President, but we have no way of knowing," he said. "We don't even remember him."

Just as appalling is the number of teenagers who, in the manner of Hinckley, have been turning to hand-guns for violence and kicks. In 1981 a CBS television special reported from Los Angeles on the terrifying handgun culture that has sprung up among the under-eighteen generation. A policeman there spoke, with some trepidation, about "fourteen-year-olds carrying .38 revolvers." A criminal-court judge spoke, with a mixture of astonishment and resignation, about kids "carrying guns to school like we used to carry ciga-rettes." These youngsters—who steal their weapons from homes and gun stores or buy them cheap in the streets—kill with little or no provocation and with hardly a sign of remorse. "You're afraid to go to work," one woman testified. "You're afraid to go to church. You're afraid to go to school. You're afraid to look at somebody, because occasionally they'll tell you, 'I don't like the way you look at me.'" Ed Bradley, the CBS correspondent, was moved to describe them as "the most violent and disturbing generation this country has ever spawned."

What made them take so casually and so violently to handguns? "Kids are growing cold," one adult resident told Bradley. "They're growing older and colder. They have no home raising, have no love." The criminal-court judge offered the opinion that such kids "have no stake whatever in society"—that "they think nothing's here for me." And according to a mental-health

worker, "by sixteen years of age a kid will have witnessed close to 18,000 murders on television." But the
gun-happy teenagers had explanations of their own.
One said, "The person with the gun got the best hand
. . . calling the shots. . . . You can just take your finger
and pull the trigger, you ain't got to worry about the
fellow no more. Bang, bang, bang, bang! You got this
fool. . . . You're kind of happy." One cited the example
of the movies: "So everybody gets a gun to figure, hey,
I got the same equal rights as another man. . . . It's like
a little Western. Let's go shoot 'em up. . . . Bam, bam,
bam, bam! It's over." And another acknowledged the
influence of television: "It's not hard to kill somebody. . . . It takes a little kid to pull the trigger. . . . I like
the feel of a gun. . . . And just the idea of pushing the
shells in. . . . I guess a lot of it comes from TV. . . . Just
watch them dudes pack their guns, and I'm ready."

It all led the Assistant District Attorney of Los Angeles to conclude that "firearms are by far and away the
most identifiable cause of violence," that "there are too
many guns in our community," and that "there are too
many people willing to use them." Moreover, there's
no sign that people will be less trigger-happy any time
soon. One of the teenagers ventured to say, "I don't
think it's ever going to stop." Such a statement might
have had a strong influence on Ed Bradley's disquieting
summation: "We may see authoritarian measures that
threaten the principles of democracy." That is an im-
probable development, however, if the present state of
mind in Washington is any indication. The authoritarian antigun impulse is unlikely to seize a United States

Congress the majority of which now curtsies as rever-
ently as it does to the nation's gun lobby—a Congress
that appears to have lost the will it once had to impose
controls on the distribution and ownership of firearms.

3

IN 1934, Congress passed the National Firearms Act,
aimed at curbing the sales of shotguns and submachine
guns, which were then among the main tools of the
gangster underworld. In 1938 it went further, passing
the Federal Firearms Act, which prohibited unlicensed
gun dealers from selling across state lines, and made it
illegal for firearms to be sold to felons and fugitives
from justice. Thirty years later, when the country was
aroused by a rash of political assassinations—the Kenne-
dys, King, Malcolm X—Congress passed the Gun Control Act of 1968. By then, the pro-gun lobby was
becoming an organized force, and had started to intimi-
date congressmen with its power to mobilize grass-
roots votes for or against political candidates. Its
influence was strong enough in 1968 to make the Gun
Control Act weaker than the bill that had been drafted
for passage: a number of the bill's provisions were wa-
tered down in the course of debate, when certain congressmen began quaking before the threats and
objections of the pro-gun lobby. Even so, the 1968 act
was the strongest that had yet been passed. Its major

provisions included a ban on the importation of handguns and on their sale to minors, drug addicts, and convicted felons. But the act would be only as effective as its loopholes—no secret to those legislators who had fought to put the loopholes in. For instance, a number of the pro-gun congressmen had assented to the clause banning the importation of handguns simply because they knew how cunningly it could be circumvented. The gun dealers whose interests they represented knew that even better. And the ink on the 1968 act was hardly dry before those dealers—complying "conscientiously" with the ban on handgun importation—began importing handgun *parts* and assembling them in the United States. Most were assembled in Florida, which is now the main center for the production of cheap Saturday Night Specials. So, despite the 1968 act, small arms have been as available as they ever were, civilian gun violence has increased, and the death rate by handguns has continued to rise.

What has also continued in America is a division of opinion over the question of gun violence—whether there is a connection between the easy availability of handguns and the increasing rates of handgun crime and murder. A large and influential segment of the population, including President Reagan, recognizes no such connection. It isn't guns that kill and commit crimes, they repeat, but people.

At one of the President's press conferences in 1983, a reporter asked, "You are aware, I'm sure, that the United States has an utterly disgraceful number of murders. Do you believe that there is any correlation between the wide dissemination of guns in this country and this disgraceful record? And, in short, isn't it time for a truly effective gun-control law?"

The President replied, "We get back to the old argument again, and I have stated many times, you cannot find in the various states that have gun-control laws that there is any proportionate difference in the crimes committed where there are those very strict laws and where they are far looser in their laws. . . . What we should be aiming at all over the country is what we did in California. And that is that never mind whether you're going to try to take guns away from the good people, the criminal is going to find a way to have a gun. What we did was to say that anyone convicted of a crime, if he had a gun in his possession at the time it was committed, whether he used it or not, add fifteen years to the prison sentence and make the prison sentence mandatory. No probation could be given. And I think that is more of an answer. The guns aren't making people criminals. Criminals are using guns."

There's strong and respectable support for the President's views, and it comes not only from within the community that is predictably pro-gun in sentiment but also from disinterested quarters of scholarship. In a study of gun use and availability conducted in the early 1980s, the sociologists James Wright and Peter Rossi, of the University of Massachusetts, arrived at this finding: "There appear to be no strong causal connections between private gun ownership and the crime rate. . . .

There is no compelling evidence that private weaponry is an important cause of, or deterrent to, violent criminality."

On the other hand, scientific polls continue to show, as they have shown for decades, that most Americans see a connection between the availability of firearms and the rate of gun crimes, and that they want much stricter controls on the circulation and possession of handguns. That constituency is not without *its* support in disinterested quarters of scholarship, for several other social-science studies have indicated that fewer handguns in the society would in all likelihood result in fewer gun crimes. So have statements by many law-enforcement officers across the nation, and so have federal statistics. The President ignored those statistics—if he knew about them—when he spoke of the "difference in the crimes committed where there are those very strict laws and where they are far looser in their laws." (Part of what that standard pro-gun rhetoric usually refers to is New York State's Sullivan Law, which is one of the oldest and strictest gun statutes in the country, and which has been a popular target for those who argue that gun laws don't work. But that argument overlooks the fact that most illegal handguns in New York are purchased in states where there are looser gun laws, or from residents of such states who smuggle handguns into New York and sell them here.) The President might not have read the F.B.I. Crime Reports for 1981, which disclose the following: "The Southern states accounted for 43 percent of the murders. The Western states reported 20 percent; the North Central states recorded 19 percent; and the Northeastern states, 17 percent." The only point the F.B.I. report failed to make, since crime statistics are its main interest, is that the Northeastern states, with the lowest murder rates cited, also have the toughest gun laws in the country. Nor does it seem, from what the 1981 CBS documentary revealed about teenage gun violence in Los Angeles, that the tough prison sentences enacted during Mr. Reagan's tenure as governor are having the deterrent effect they were intended to have.

Since the early 1970s, when it became clear that dealers were circumventing the Gun Control Act of 1968, a number of bills have been introduced in Congress to close the loopholes and stiffen the act. Almost all have died or been snarled in committee. Pro-gun legislators not only helped to stymie those bills but also introduced some of their own, intended to crush from the 1968 act whatever real force it still had. As this is written, there are two major gun bills, one from each camp, that remain in committee while their leading sponsors and strategists maneuver for enough votes to strengthen their chances of passage on the floors of the House and the Senate. One of them, whose co-authors are Senator Edward Kennedy and Representative Peter Rodino, proposes a ban on the domestic manufacture of cheap handguns and on the importation of parts that are used to assemble Saturday Night Specials. The other, whose co-authors are Senator James McClure and Representative Harold Volkmer, and which is known as the Firearm Owners Protection Act, seeks, in effect, to pull whatever teeth are left in the Gun Control Act of 1968.

Kennedy-Rodino can count on a slight majority in the Democratic-controlled House, whereas a majority in the Republican-controlled Senate leans toward McClure-Volkmer—a bill that President Reagan has promised to sign if it comes to his desk. As a 1982 Senate document states: "Thus there remains a clear division in Congress between advocates of an interdiction solution—a policy that seeks to lessen the likelihood and danger of crime by curbing access to the more lethal weapons—and those who believe the problem is one of establishing a more effective system of criminal justice. The former see the easy availability of firearms as a principal generator of crime. The latter insist that the proper focal point is the offender and that any workmanlike solution lies in the principles of deterrence and appropriate sentencing." This division in Congress, of course, reflects the division in the nation as a whole— one constituency backing the aims of Kennedy-Rodino, and the other solidly behind the purposes of McClure-Volkmer.

4

THE CONSTITUENCY supporting the Kennedy-Rodino bill is represented chiefly by the two leading antigun organizations in America—the National Coalition to Ban Handguns and Handgun Control, Inc., both with headquarters in Washington. The National Coalition, the smaller of the two, is headed by Michael Beard, a former legislative aide. It is co-sponsored by over thirty religious, labor, political, and civic groups, and its advisory council has included Eugene Carson Blake, Leonard Bernstein, Julian Bond, Harvey Cox, Robert Drinan, James Farmer, Walter Fauntroy, John Kenneth Galbraith, and Norman Lear. Despite its smaller size, the National Coalition makes an even tougher demand than Handgun Control, Inc., does: rather than a limitation on the production and circulation of handguns, which is what Handgun Control, Inc., seeks, it wants a total ban on the production and possession of handguns, whether cheap or expensive, imported or domestically made. Beard told an interviewer in 1981, "We remain convinced that nothing short of an outright ban on civilian possession of handguns will ultimately be effective in reducing handgun crime and saving lives. If you call a total ban extreme, then we're extremists." Therefore, while the National Coalition lobbies strongly against the McClure-Volkmer bill, it isn't as enthusiastic about Kennedy-Rodino as it would be if that bill were also seeking a total ban on the production and possession of handguns. The cheap handgun remains "an easy target for legislators," Beard argues, "because the very name conjures up an image of the proverbial poor, inner-city youth, or petty criminal buying one for fifty bucks on a street corner." He maintains that "a larger problem is now posed by the high-quality $200 to $300 handgun purchased by the white, blue-collar homeowner in the suburbs and stashed in a dresser drawer for 'self-protection.' " And though he feels no animosity against Handgun Control, Inc., he nevertheless asks, "Does it make sense to spend so much time and money pushing for a national handgun-control bill, given that its chances are so poor?" Of course, there's enough evidence to suggest that if the push were for a total ban, its chances would be even poorer.

"Gun control has been a great liberal cause," a New York City gun buff scoffed some time ago, going on to say that liberals "are not for strict controls, they are just not for any guns at all." Neither part of his statement is strictly true. Though gun regulation *has* been a liberal cause, it has not been a cause for all liberals: there are liberals who want strict controls, and nothing more; there are liberals who want no guns at all; and there are liberals who want no controls at all. There are also gun-control advocates who have nothing liberal in their personal or political backgrounds. One such anomaly is Nelson (Pete) Shields, who leads Handgun Control, Inc. Shields was an executive for E. I. du Pont before he joined the antigun movement. He had been a Republican all his life, and a devoted hunter as well. And he still has no objections to shotguns and rifles. He hates handguns, however. It was the loss of one of his children to a handgun wielder that drove him into the work he's now doing.

In 1975, after his son Nick had been killed on a street in San Francisco by a member of a gang of gunmen known as Zebras, who were then terrorizing the city, Shields quit his job at Du Pont and began helping out a small and underfinanced group in Washington called the National Council to Control Handguns. His son's murder, he has explained, "made me wonder whether I could do something to stop this from happening to somebody else's kid." In 1976 he became the chairman of the National Council, which changed its name to Handgun Control, Inc., two years later, and has grown to be the largest organization of its kind in the country. Handgun Control, Inc., now has what it calls a "citizen army" of seven hundred and fifty thousand members, about a hundred and fifty thousand of whom contribute to its operating budget ($2.3 million in 1982). Its national-committee members have included Steve Allen, Arthur Ashe, Leonard Bernstein, Ellen Burstyn, Edmund G. Brown, Sr., Mayors Kenneth Gibson and Richard Hatcher, Martin Luther King, Sr., Peter Lawford, John Lindsay, and William Ruckelshaus. Like the pro-gun movement that it fights, Handgun Control, Inc., lobbies in Congress, aids gun-control groups in local communities, endorses politicians who endorse its objectives, and opposes those who oppose them. An example of the last of these activities is a piece of mail that it sent to New York voters in 1982: "Why . . . is our new Senator, Alphonse D'Amato, co-sponsoring a bill [McClure-Volkmer] to weaken our national law? . . . Why is Senator D'Amato proposing that we begin erasing EVERY federal gun law on the books? . . . Mr. D'Amato has no business sponsoring a bill that endangers the lives of the very people he represents. . . . Why did he do it? Perhaps it's because he received $16,259 from the National Rifle Association's Political Victory Fund in the last election." Voters in New York cannot have been the only ones who received such a message, for D'Amato is surely not the only senator backing the McClure-Volkmer bill. Nor was his senatorial campaign the only one that took money from the N.R.A. In any event, the letter to New Yorkers is an example of what and how Handgun Control, Inc., has learned from its powerful N.R.A.-led opposition, for it reflects a technique—direct mass mailing—that that gun lobby has perfected and has used to mobilize formidable support for its cause.

The pro-gun lobby—a giant compared to Handgun Control, Inc.—is one of the largest, strongest, and best-financed special-interest groups in the nation's capital. Made up of organizations on the far right—the more prominent ones being the Second Amendment Foundation, the Citizens Committee for the Right to Keep and Bear Arms, and the National Rifle Association—it seeks to preserve for its adherents, and for other Americans as well, their right to own firearms. It regards all gun-control advocates as "gun grabbers"—as people whose true objective is not to regulate the possession of firearms but to confiscate all guns. It spreads that belief among its grass-roots following, and scares members of Congress with its ability to organize that belief and translate it into a mass of pro-gun votes.

Though polls show that the gun lobby represents a minority opinion in the United States, its membership far outnumbers that of the antigun organizations, and it has managed to exercise something resembling a veto over the desire that most Americans have expressed for stronger gun laws. This may be because the opponents of gun control are better organized—and perhaps more organizable—than the proponents. It may also be that they are seldom critical of their leadership, and do not hesitate at election time to put their votes where their gun convictions are. Many gun-control advocates, on the other hand, even those who are organized, do not, as a rule, vote solely on the issue of guns—they won't work to elect or defeat a candidate just because of his position on firearms. So while they continue to hope for stronger gun laws they help to frustrate their own hopes by maintaining an admirable civic attitude: by continuing to act on the principle that a candidate's stand on a range of national and international issues provides a fairer test of his credentials for office than whether he's likely to support or oppose gun-control measures.

The Second Amendment Foundation and the Citizens Committee for the Right to Keep and Bear Arms are sister organizations. They share an address (in the state of Washington, though only the Committee maintains lobbyists on Capitol Hill) and a number of the same officers; for instance, Alan Gottlieb, the founder and chairman of the Citizens Committee, is also the president of the Second Amendment Foundation. The Citizens Committee is the larger and more politically active of the two, and its advisory board includes more than a hundred and fifty United States senators and representatives—a sign of its influence in the corridors of Congress. Though the Citizens Committee isn't the major force in the gun lobby, it's a formidable one. Its

1981 report states: "Members and supporters have multiplied from less than 9,000 when we began [in 1971] to a figure that may well hit the half-million mark by the end of 1982," and adds, "This year we will spend well over a million dollars lobbying in Congress and state legislatures and on more than twenty-five projects, with only one goal in mind: the preservation of our RIGHT to keep and bear arms."

The National Rifle Association, thanks to the size of its following, the size of its treasury, and the strength of its clout in Congress, is the undisputed champion of the pro-gun lobby. It has a membership of over two and a half million, while that of its chief opponent, Handgun Control, Inc., is less than a third as large. And in 1982 its treasury financed a budget of $36 million, compared to $2.3 million spent that year by Handgun Control, Inc. A 1983 issue of *Reports from Washington,* which is published by the N.R.A., says: "The National Rifle Association spent more money communicating with association members during the 1981–1982 election year than did any other organization in America, according to figures released . . . by the Federal Election Commission. The F.E.C. examinations . . . show the N.R.A. spent $803,656 on literature and other types of information designed to acquaint . . . members with the policies of various candidates in the federal election races. . . . One group not listed in the report was Handgun Control, Inc. . . . But H.C.I.'s [Political Action Committee] gave more than $50,000 directly to candidates with pro-gun–control sentiments, according to F.E.C. documents."

One resemblance between these two rivals is that

each is led by a man whose life has been marked by the tragedy of gunfire, but that resemblance only reflects the contrasting interests and characters of the two organizations. Nelson Shields came to Handgun Control, Inc., after his son was killed by a gunman; and Harlon Carter took over the N.R.A. leadership decades after he was tried for the shooting and killing of a Mexican-American in Texas, his native state. The incident occurred in 1931, when Carter and his victim were teenagers, and it gained no wide attention until 1981, when—Carter having become a luminary of the pro-gun movement—the Laredo *Times* dug the story from its files and reprinted it. According to the story, Carter was sentenced to three years in jail but was released when a state appeals court ruled that the witnesses against him were untrustworthy. In 1982, while the N.R.A. was holding an annual convention in Philadelphia, that city's *Inquirer* also ran the old story of the shooting incident. But if it was news to the assembly of N.R.A. delegates, it did nothing to alter the high esteem in which they held their leader. Nor did it moderate Carter's militant rhetoric on behalf of the right to own and use guns. "We can reasonably and rightfully . . . aspire to a time when few politicians, mindful of their futures, will oppose us," he told the delegates. "Don't trust a politician who won't trust you with a gun."

If one of the original members of the N.R.A. had got up to make such statements at an annual meeting, or any other kind of meeting, of its members, he might have been regarded as a lunatic, or else might have been asked to take himself and his views to a more appropriate organization. The N.R.A. was anything but a gun lobby when it came into being, in 1871. For decades after its founding—in cosmopolitan New York, of all places—its main and almost its sole purpose was the teaching of long-range marksmanship to the post–Civil War generation of riflemen. In the early years of this century, having moved its headquarters to Washington, D.C., it became an organization for hunters, farmers, ranchers, sports shooters, and gun collectors, and a sponsor of rifle clubs and target-shooting contests around the nation. This essentially sporting and practical group of gun fanciers became politicized, and radically so, during the 1960s, when the political assassinations and race riots of that decade and the proliferation of gun crimes reawoke public anxiety over the destructiveness of firearms in American life. That anxiety was one of the main forces behind the passage of the 1968 Gun Control Act, and the passage of that act hastened the transformation of the N.R.A. into a militant advocate and defender of gun-owning rights.

Since then, the N.R.A. has led the fight against almost all attempts to pass stricter gun laws. In 1980 it took the unprecedented step of endorsing a candidate for President, and has claimed credit for millions of the votes that put Mr. Reagan in the White House. That year, too, through its Institute for Legislative Action, it spent more than $1 million to help elect pro-gun candidates; and the conservative landslide to which it contributed strengthened its position not only in the White House but in Congress as well. Drawing inspiration and justification from the Second Amendment to the Constitution of the United States, it views as sacrosanct the civilian right to own and use guns. Further, it sees the exercise of that right as a potential defense against any repressive or authoritarian government that might one day arise in the United States. That is the point the N.R.A. was making in the full-page newspaper ads it ran after Lech Walesa and the Solidarity movement had been crushed. "The actions of the Polish Government in suspending basic rights and liberties of its citizens should cause every American to say a silent thank you for the foresight of the drafters of the U.S. Constitution," the ad told Polish-Americans. "Poland has precisely the firearms laws that the N.R.A. has been opposing in the United States. . . . And so long as the Second Amendment is not infringed what is happening in Poland can never happen in the United States."

5

"THE RIGHT TO KEEP AND BEAR ARMS" is only one of a number of slogans by which the N.R.A. and its allies make their case against gun-control legislation. Others, proclaimed from bumper stickers across the nation, are Gun Laws Don't Work, If Guns Are Outlawed Only Outlaws Will Have Guns, Registration Is the First Step to Confiscation, and, of course, Guns Don't Kill, People Do. These slogans are also the basis of pamphlets, letters to the faithful, newspaper ads, speeches, and articles in the gun press, and of Alan Gottlieb's book *The Rights of Gun Owners*—a bible of the pro-gun movement. Gottlieb speaks outside the pages of his book as well. "For over a decade," he has told an interviewer, "law-abiding Americans who own guns for legitimate purposes have been blamed by political hacks and extreme leftist media ideologues for rising rates of crime in our country, when the real cause for the rates is the permissive, mealy-mouthed, mollycoddling attitude of these same hacks and ideologues." In "Anti-Gunners Are a Threat to America," an article published in a 1982 issue of *Guns & Ammo,* the writer Bill Clede maintains, "Pro-gunners are in favor of gun control. They want to eliminate plea bargaining of gun charges against criminals. They do *not* favor proposed laws that harass the honest citizen while having no effect on crime. . . . So, if the anti-gunners win, we 'the people' have no right to peaceably assemble, maintain personal security, retain rights not delegated by the federal government, or keep and bear arms. As far as I'm concerned, the greatest threat of all this furor over 'gun control' has nothing to do with guns. It is a threat to my country and the democratic principles I believe in."

Gun-control advocates, for their part, wonder why the gun lobbyists resist so strenuously virtually every attempt to regulate the manufacture, circulation, possession, and use of handguns. Why, since even they, the antigunners, do not wish to proscribe the rights of long-gun owners, does the pro-gun lobby oppose the slightest restriction on the production and use of snubbies— the weapons that account for so many of the gun murders and other gun crimes in the United States? In 1981 the Reverend James Hickey, the Roman Catholic Bishop of Washington, found himself being denounced by the Citizens Committee for the Right to Keep and Bear Arms as a member of the "gun-grabbing" clergy. The Reverend Mr. Hickey had said that he dearly wished to see "the elimination of handguns from society." What could have been so evil about the Bishop's wish? Answers to that question may or may not be found in something that Alan Gottlieb has said against the movement to ban cheap handguns: "One compelling argument against such a ban has been brought forward by Ernest Van den Haag. He reasons that the poor and the elderly are the chief victims of crime and cannot necessarily afford expensive handguns for self-defense, and since inner-city police protection is so poor, many citizens must rely on self-protection."

Another question is raised by the stand that the pro-gun lobby has taken on the subject of armor-piercing bullets. They are also known as "cop-killer bullets," since they are designed to penetrate bullet-resistant vests, worn mainly by the police. Eight types of armor-piercing bullets have been identified—five imported and three manufactured over here. The most powerful and devastating are coated with Teflon: they can penetrate the equivalent of four vests lined with seventy-two layers of bullet-resistant Kevlar. Why has the N.R.A. fought efforts to restrict their sales? In a letter to the *Times* in June 1982, the head of New York's Police Foundation protested the N.R.A. stand:

Why are these bullets being manufactured? In my judgment, and in the judgment of the police community, they are purchased mainly to penetrate bullet-proof vests worn by police officers.

Two bills to study the matter of penetration of bullet-proof vests and to prohibit manufacture of these bullets have been introduced in the House of Representatives. . . . At present, they appear to have little chance of passage because both the National Rifle Association and the Reagan Administration refuse to place any restriction on ammunition.

I can think of no single issue in criminal justice that should compel more unequivocal public support than restricting these bullets. . . .

The criminals using them are the most desperate and the most odious. . . . With the killer bullet, they have a guarantee they can mortally wound anyone they wish, vest or not.

The slogan of the N.R.A. people flies in their face on this issue. Their argument that "if you outlaw guns, only the outlaws will have them" cannot be true for killer bullets, because if they were outlawed only certain law enforcement officers would have them. I believe the police would give them up completely if this would eliminate unauthorized use.

There is one happy note: Du Pont . . . has taken the courageous stand that it will not sell Teflon to bullet manufacturers who intend to make "killer" bullets. The company is to be congratulated for the highest level of corporate responsibility in resisting the pressure of the manufacturers and the N.R.A.

It is not only in Congress and in the big cities that the N.R.A. has fought to keep Teflon-coated bullets in circulation. As Steve Burke, a councilman for the town of

Brookhaven in New York's Suffolk County, can testify,
the N.R.A. has fought in small communities as well.
Burke, the father of a policeman in New York City, had
occasion, in 1982, to reflect on the problem of Teflon-
coated bullets, his son having said that it worried him
to think he might still be shot dead, despite the "safety
blanket," or bulletproof vest, that he wore. After considering the matter for some time, the older Burke—
though he was powerless to protect his son in New York
City—began thinking of what he could do to protect
the policemen in Brookhaven; and in a talk with the
town supervisor he suggested that a law be passed in
Brookhaven banning the sale of Teflon-coated bullets.
The supervisor replied that she could imagine no one
objecting to such a law. "Who would be for bullets that
can pierce armor and kill cops?" she asked. "Well, nobody I can think of," Councilman Burke said. But there
were people in the community he hadn't thought of.
He introduced his bill, and before public hearings could
be held on it he received a letter from an N.R.A. member objecting to the proposed law and informing him
that the N.R.A. would fight it to the bitter end. It wasn't
an empty threat. A flood of letters and telephone calls
started coming in, and N.R.A. adherents turned out in
large and vociferous numbers when the public hearings
began. One of them got up and shouted at the town
legislators, "You call yourselves Americans, voting for
this? You ought to be ashamed, whoever brought this
damn law up. It's a real shame. Americans! You want to
restrict our rights!" When a local policeman was
granted a hearing, he said this: "Our police officers in

Suffolk County and indeed throughout the country must be assured that our law-abiding citizens are in their corner. We are human beings. We are not machines. We cry when we're hurt. We bleed when we're cut. And we die when we're shot." Burke's bill was eventually enacted, over the not-quite-dead body of the N.R.A. Fighting to the bitter end, as it had promised, the N.R.A. opposition took its case to the Suffolk County Council, whose authority overrides that of any locality within its jurisdiction, and obtained a law rescinding the one passed in Brookhaven. This law permitted the continued sale of armor-piercing bullets in the county and provided that possession of such bullets would be punishable only if they were used in the commission of a crime; that is, only if they were used to injure or to kill. It was characteristic of the lengths to which the gun lobby has carried its alleged right to keep and use firearms: the penalty for using those bullets was what mattered—not whether they were available, or whether lives could be saved by proscribing their sale. Of a similar case in Virginia, where N.R.A. pressure had kept Teflon-coated bullets from being outlawed, the Arlington *Journal* said in 1982: "Frankly, we're tired of the N.R.A.'s knee-jerk opposition to reasonable proposals. We can't help but believe that the organization's opposition to outlawing a weapon whose sole purpose is to kill police officers reveals the morally bankrupt nature of the group."

In 1983, Governor Charles Robb, of Virginia, signed a bill proposing strong legal penalties on anyone who was convicted of using armor-piercing bullets in the commission of a crime. The bill had passed the state legislature with the support of the N.R.A., and, according to Warren Cassidy, the executive director of the N.R.A.'s Institute for Legislative Action, Robb's signature reemphasized "the concept that law-abiding gun owners have rights and responsibilities and that criminals should be held fully accountable for their actions." The N.R.A. continued to oppose any limitation on the freedom to acquire such bullets. Eleven states—Alabama, California, Florida, Illinois, Indiana, Kansas, Minnesota, Oklahoma, Rhode Island, Texas, and Virginia—have legislated, in one form or another, against cop-killer bullets. At the national level, however, attempts to curb their distribution have had no success. Senator Daniel Patrick Moynihan and Representative Mario Biaggi have proposed legislation that would ban the manufacture, importation, sale, and use of such ammunition; but—partly because of strong lobbying efforts by the N.R.A.—their bill (the Law Enforcement Officers Protection Act) has been stalled in committee since 1981, when it was introduced. According to an article by Representative Biaggi that appeared in *Law Enforcement News* in December of 1983, there are two major reasons that his proposed legislation has yet to be enacted: "First, the National Rifle Association strongly opposes a ban on armor-piercing handgun ammunition. Second, the Reagan Administration, while not opposed to the idea, has offered very little meaningful support for such a ban." Jerry Kenney, a pro-gun and pro-hunting writer for the New York *Daily News,* had this to say in one of his columns during March of 1984:

The image of the sportsman, the average law-abiding hunter and target shooter, is going to suffer greatly from a puzzling decision by the National Rifle Association. This august (until now) organization, which claims to be the "voice" of law-abiding gun owners in the U.S., is opposing a bill by Rep. Mario Biaggi and Sen. Daniel Patrick Moynihan that would ban the production, import, sale and private use of armor-piercing bullets.

Hunters and target shooters have traditionally been known as sportsmen and most of them are members of the N.R.A. They stand by the organization in most of its decisions, particularly in the campaign against gun control. But the stand the N.R.A. is taking in the name of its many millions of members to allow the production and sale of ammunition that has no logical use except to penetrate armor and bulletproof vests is an outrage. . . .

It seems to me if the N.R.A. doesn't support a ban of the bullets it will share the responsibility for the damage. That responsibility will trickle down to all its members, anyone who displays an N.R.A. sticker on his car windshield or wears an N.R.A. hat or carries an N.R.A. card. And I don't think N.R.A. members want it on their consciences. I know I don't.

To the N.R.A. there was no such thing as a good bullet or a bad bullet. Hence the organization viewed the Biaggi-Moynihan bill as a kind of Trojan Horse, waiting to invade the rights of all gun owners, to deprive them of all ammunition. That was not, of course, the intent of the proposed legislation. Its main intent was to ban the circulation of Teflon-coated bullets used in handguns, the ammunition and the weapons that are most deadly to law-enforcement officers. Biaggi, a former New York City policeman, who had been wounded several times in the line of duty, had more than just an antigun interest in the legislation he proposed. And Moynihan reemphasized to the Senate, in April of 1984, "Time and again Congressman Biaggi and I have stressed that only bullets capable of penetrating body armor and designed to be fired from a handgun would be banned; rifle ammunition would not be covered." The N.R.A. was not persuaded by such a statement, however. Therefore, recognizing the N.R.A.'s fears— and deciding that softer legislation was better than no legislation at all—Biaggi rewrote sections of his bill to make it explicit that certain vital interests of the pro-gun lobby would not be threatened. He was then able, in June of 1984, to write reassuringly to his congressional colleagues that the amended legislation would not infringe upon "the rights of sportsmen and other legitimate gun owners"; that it was developed jointly with the Treasury and Justice departments; that it was supported by the law-enforcement community; and that "even the N.R.A. has informed the Administration they will not oppose it." So, barring a change of heart, before or after this is published, the N.R.A. and the Reagan Administration will give their support to the Biaggi-Moynihan bill, banning the circulation of cop-killer bullets.

The pro-gun convictions of the N.R.A. are anchored in rights that it claims Americans have been granted by the Constitution of the United States. An N.R.A. man said during the hearings in Brookhaven, "When you open a loophole with a law like this, you're just . . .

unplugging a dike; you take your finger out of the hole and it's an approach, and eventually it erodes away everything, and we all go down the tubes." He was clearly referring to the Second Amendment, which states: "A well regulated militia being necessary to the security of a free state, the right of the people to keep and bear arms shall not be infringed."

It is the principal clause of the Second Amendment that the gun lobby lives by. Its words adorn the letterheads of the Citizens Committee for the Right to Keep and Bear Arms and are inscribed in stone on the building that the N.R.A. owns and occupies in the nation's capital. The gun-control movement, disagreeing with the gun lobby's interpretation of that clause, has preferred to look at the full wording of the amendment. So has the Supreme Court of the United States, which ruled in 1939 (and has since declined to reconsider the matter) that the Second Amendment applies to the maintenance of a well-regulated militia, and not to any individual's right to keep and bear arms. Federal courts have abided by that ruling, and in 1975 the American Bar Association stated that the Second Amendment and similar provisions in state constitutions "have never prevented regulation of firearms."

Such opinions have failed to impress or influence the pro-gun leadership. It has continued to ignore or play down the Second Amendment's reference to a militia, or, by niceties of historical interpretation, has sought to bend the meaning to its own interests. In 1982 the Senate Subcommittee on the Constitution—chaired by Orrin G. Hatch, who is on the advisory council of the

Citizens Committee for the Right to Keep and Bear Arms—claimed to have found enough evidence in Colonial writings and in modern testimony to justify an "individual" rather than a strictly "militia" reading of the Second Amendment. "What the Subcommittee . . . uncovered," Senator Hatch said in a preface to his committee's report, "was clear—and long-lost—proof that the Second Amendment to our Constitution was intended as an individual right of the American citizen to keep and carry arms in a peaceful manner, for protection of himself, his family, and his freedoms." Naturally, such a finding was profoundly reassuring to leaders of the pro-gun lobby. It quickened their hope that the Supreme Court might one day—perhaps soon —reverse itself on the Second Amendment, as it has done on a number of other constitutional questions.

6

AFTER THE CONSERVATIVE LANDSLIDE of 1980 boosted the pro-gun position on Capitol Hill and in the White House, prospects for new gun-control legislation seemed bleaker than ever. If most Americans still wanted stricter gun laws, it looked as though they would have to pass those laws themselves, at the state and local levels. It probably looked that way to the people of Morton Grove, a small town in Illinois, for in June of 1981, not many months after the pro-gun conservatives were swept into Washington, Morton Grove attracted national headlines by banning the private possession of handguns within the town limits.

That initiative—probably the toughest and most un-compromising gun law that had yet been passed in America—couldn't have come from a less likely com-munity. Though Morton Grove is only sixteen miles from downtown Chicago, it is a quiet residential sub-urb. Its population is twenty-four thousand, and it has just two streets for shopping, the rest being lined mostly with single-family houses. Gun crimes were not unknown in the community, but they were never much of a problem, and certainly were never prevalent among its citizens. Neil Cashman was then the senior governing trustee of Morton Grove, and, with white hair and a sober avuncular manner, he looked the part. A law like Morton Grove's "had to start somewhere," Cashman said later. "Why not here?" But it wasn't to set an example for the rest of the country that he intro-duced the bill that became law. He was simply trying to prevent Morton Grove—and especially its younger citizens—from developing too great a feeling for hand-guns. One resident had applied to the trustees for per-mission to open a gun store, on a site not far from the town's junior high school. "We didn't want the kids looking in the window, dreaming of guns," Cashman has said. "We wanted to stop that store." Since there were no legal grounds on which permission could be denied—no federal or state law, no local zoning statute —the trustees could stop that store only by outlawing the sale and private possession of handguns in their town; and on June 8, 1981, they passed an ordinance doing just that. Residents were required to surrender their handguns to the police or to stash them in gun clubs beyond the town limits. The trustees—realizing, perhaps, the national import of their action—then took two further steps. They voted to make copies of their ordinance available to any governmental body in the nation that requested them, and also passed this resolution: "That all other municipalities, counties, and states in the United States and the U.S. Congress legislate against the manufacture, importation, sale and private possession of handguns, except for use by law enforcement and security personnel, military and sportsmen's clubs."

Morton Grove's ordinance, reported prominently in the press and on television, stirred a national response. Of course, not all of it was favorable. Among the letters that poured into the offices of the trustees from across America were some addressed to "Moron Grove" or "Morton Grave"—and what their writers thought of the town's antigun law was couched in terms like "Nazi," "Communist," "vile," and "filthy." The letters commending Morton Grove for its action included some from towns and localities that wished to adopt the ordinance as a model for gun-control legislation of their own. And within months stricter gun measures—some adhering to the letter of Morton Grove's, others merely reflecting its spirit—were proposed in cities like Chicago, San Francisco, Los Angeles, and East St. Louis,

Illinois, and in several smaller municipalities. Neil Cashman's idea clearly seemed to be catching on around the nation.

Morton Grove had taken the N.R.A. off guard. When the N.R.A. got wind of Cashman's proposal, just before it was debated and passed, the organization swung into its usual oppositionist action, orchestrating its usual avalanche of letters and phone calls. It was too late. Minds in Morton Grove—the majority, anyway—were already made up. Defeated by this fait accompli, an experience to which they were unaccustomed, the national pro-gun leaders sought to overturn the Morton Grove ban by challenging its constitutionality before the federal and local courts of Illinois. But judicial opinion was firmly against them. In December of 1981 the United States District Court of Northern Illinois ruled that the Morton Grove ordinance violated neither the federal Constitution nor the constitution of the state of Illinois. In January of 1982 the circuit court of Cook County held that Morton Grove's ordinance infringed upon no guarantees of the Illinois constitution. In December of that year the United States Court of Appeals in Chicago upheld the ruling made by the federal district court in 1981. And in March of 1983 the Court of Appeals again ruled in favor of the ordinance. This last ruling was a severe blow to the pro-gun lobby, which had helped to lead and finance the court challenges, for it had now exhausted its appeals at all levels below the Supreme Court of the United States. The pro-gun movement vowed to take its fight all the way to the Supreme Court of the United States—for, according to one of its spokesmen, the movement regarded the Morton Grove law as "the most dangerous attack ever staged against the right to bear arms." Obviously, that right hadn't appealed very strongly to the trustees and citizens of Morton Grove. They seem to have felt more strongly about their right to fear arms and their right to inscribe that fear in the democratic arrangements by which they govern themselves. Part of their motivation may be inferred from an article that one of the trustees later wrote for a Chicago newspaper. "What happened in Morton Grove is not extraordinary," he said. "It was, in fact, a textbook civics exercise in American government at its best."

Morton Grove provided the national gun-control movement with an impressive victory, even though the leaders of that movement may have been taken just as much unawares as the N.R.A. was. Michael Beard, of the National Coalition to Ban Handguns, called it "a symbolic message that is being sent to public officials that they can do something about handgun problems." And in view of the number of communities that followed Morton Grove's lead, public officials had not ignored the message. An even more striking development—though one cannot be sure how much of it was influenced by Morton Grove—was a new and audacious front that private citizens opened in the gun-control battle. In February of 1982 a jury in Washington, D.C., awarded $2 million to the family of a man who had been shot and killed with a pistol stolen from the N.R.A.'s headquarters. (The award was later set aside, when a United States district court judge ruled that the

N.R.A. could not be held legally responsible for the murder.) A few months later, James Brady, the White House press secretary who was critically wounded in John Hinckley's attack on President Reagan, filed a $100 million damage claim against the manufacturer of Hinckley's Saturday Night Special. And by the summer of 1982 Windle Turley—a Dallas lawyer who had helped initiate the new product-liability strategy—had filed more than a dozen suits seeking to hold handgun-makers liable for murders and felonious injuries committed with the weapons they produced.

But Michael Beard had also asserted that Morton Grove "clearly marks a turning point" in the national struggle for handgun-control laws, and that was over-optimistic. The evidence since then (except for court rulings on the Morton Grove ordinance) has failed to support his judgment. There has been no sign yet that the message from Morton Grove was heard in the Congress of the United States. Morton Grove hasn't noticeably improved the chances of the Kennedy-Rodino handgun-control bill, and it hasn't diminished support for McClure-Volkmer, the bill seeking to further weaken the Gun Control Act of 1968. A ban on handguns in San Francisco, which followed Morton Grove's ban, was overturned by the state's superior courts. And, in direct rebuttal to Morton Grove and its followers in other towns, several communities have flaunted their Second Amendment "rights" by passing laws to compel their citizens to own firearms.

The first and most widely publicized of these cases was that of Kennesaw, Georgia, which, with a popula-

tion of seven thousand, was an even smaller town than
Morton Grove. In 1982, Kennesaw enacted an ordinance making it illegal for any household to be without
a gun. That went beyond the most extreme previous
pro-gun demands, and looked to many outsiders like a
copycat law in reverse, or merely a publicity stunt.
Whatever its motivation, Kennesaw and its mayor, Darvin Purdy, attracted almost as much national attention
as Morton Grove had. Not even the New York *Times*
could resist devoting an editorial to Kennesaw. Mayor
Purdy made a number of appearances on national television and also released the text of a letter he had
mailed to Mayor Dianne Feinstein, of San Francisco,
requesting that "you allow us to have your surrendered
and confiscated weapons, so that we may issue them to
our indigent citizens." But in Kennesaw itself, there
were questions about the law. Could it be enforced?
Would the head of a family be fined or imprisoned for
refusing to keep a gun in the house? Apparently not;
drafters of the law had been careful to omit any penalty
so drastic. "It's gonna be tough to enforce," the town's
police chief said soon after the ordinance was passed.
"You can't walk into people's houses and ask to see their
guns." He added, however, that Kennesaw stood ready
to "supply just about any sort of firearm" to residents
who lacked the funds to purchase their own. To some
residents of Kennesaw, the law was downright silly.
"What are they going to do next?" a local educator
asked. "Order everybody to buy a pickup truck to escape in case of a nuclear holocaust? Here we were,
trying to live down a redneck image, and they do this.

It's crazy." A businessman added, "This just makes us the laughingstock of the whole country."

Well, not of the whole country. Surely not of the pro-gun lobby, which raised Kennesaw as a flag to wave against the "morons" of Morton Grove. *Point Blank,* the newsletter of the Citizens Committee for the Right to Keep and Bear Arms, praised the Kennesaw ordinance, calling it "a solid counter" to the Morton Grove handgun ban, and added: "The fight goes on around the country." And so it was. KENNESAW-TYPE GUN LAW SPREADING LIKE WILDFIRE, declared a headline in the newspaper *Gun Week* during July 1982. Such laws "have now been passed in Kennesaw, Franklintown, Pa., Hollister, Mo., Chiloquin, Ore., and Palmer, Ill.," the accompanying story pointed out. "They are being considered in a number of towns, including Oroville, Calif., Bliss, Idaho, and Taylorville, Ill." And a number of other localities have since proposed or adopted gun codes similar to Kennesaw's. The news was a clear sign that the N.R.A. and its allies had recovered from the shock of their ambush in Morton Grove.

In September 1983, Michael Korda, a novelist and book editor in New York, wrote an article for *Reports from Washington,* the N.R.A. publication, in which he agreed substantially with the N.R.A.'s position on gun control. The association later ran Mr. Korda's article, under the heading "Guns Are Not the Problem," as an advertisement in a number of magazines, including the *New Republic*—presumably because Mr. Korda's credentials are those of an urban intellectual, because urban intellectuals are generally seen to be liberal, and because liberals are generally deemed to be in favor of gun control. As it happens, Mr. Korda is a gun collector, a target shooter, and a member of the N.R.A., but most New Yorkers, unaware of all this, were surprised to read his pro-gun statement. An article in the New York *Post* asked incredulously, "Michael Korda, novelist, editor, urbane sophisticate—and a gun freak?"

"Gun freak" is not a term that properly describes Mr. Korda, however strong his pro-gun opinions may be. Some time before the article appeared, Mr. Korda, in a conversation at his office with this writer, spelled out his views. "When people talk about guns, what are they really talking about?" he said. "They are talking about a certain American penchant for violence. They're talking about the conflict between the old rural view of American life and the modern urban view of American life. They're talking about liberal and conservative attitudes toward self-defense and crime. They're talking about crime and about standing up for their rights to the extreme. They're talking about all sorts of issues that are very intense in American life, including, I need hardly say, racism, and all of which boil down to guns and gun control. The guns themselves have never struck me as being very interesting or, in real American terms, very controversial. The truth of the matter is that when people talk about gun control they're really talking about other things. Conservatives are talking about constitutional rights. Rural people are talking about looking after themselves. Big-city people are talking about what are seen as person-to-person crimes —seen by white people as being inflicted on them largely by blacks, and seen by black people as being inflicted largely on blacks by blacks. And city people, if they're liberal, are also thinking about a certain turning away from old American values, which are basically and predominantly rural."

Mr. Korda went on to say, "What applies to a city like New York does not, it seems to me, apply as easily to a state like Montana. What applies to Montana does not apply as easily to a state like Mississippi. And local custom, local tradition, local law enforcement vary so much that it is really very hard to talk about a national gun policy—which I think everybody in the federal government does more or less badly. There is no reason to suppose that a national gun policy would be better administered than a national anything-else policy—energy policy, civil-rights policy, or whatever. So I'm not so sure that the system we have—which is that gun laws are left largely to local communities—doesn't in some ways make the most sense. And while I'm not in favor of the decision of the Morton Grove people, it seems to me that within whatever the constitutional limits turn out to be—it may well be that the Constitution does not give a community the right to mandate or to demand that it give up its guns entirely—if Morton Grove is silly, Kennesaw is sillier. The decision as to whether a person wants to arm himself or herself seems to me a very personal one, like most other things. I don't think it should be managed by the state. I don't think it should be prevented by the state. I think there's a case to be made that, given the typology of the environment, the political traditions, and so forth, of various areas, it can't be regulated by the state, just as the state regulates cars."

After a pause, Mr. Korda continued, "One of the problems I have, as a logical person, is that gun-control laws as such don't seem to do what gun-control advocates think they will do. They don't diminish homicides, reduce crime, or cut down on the number of deaths. The reason for that is that those deaths and crimes have absolutely nothing to do with gun-control laws. They have to do with poverty, urban environment, density of population, address, and so forth. We don't have a gun problem in the United States. We have a problem of violence, a problem of law enforcement, and a problem that we are absolutely unwilling to address or solve—and that problem is not guns but youth unemployment, poverty, and so forth. I feel very strongly that the crux of the problem lies in the fact that we have come to accept the criminal use of guns as natural and normal. I think it is outrageous that a guy who uses a gun in a crime should be able to plea-bargain that down to a misdemeanor. I think if you commit a crime with a gun, you ought to go up for ten years. And if you shoot or kill somebody with a gun, you should get at least a life sentence. And while I myself am not convinced that capital punishment is a good idea or a moral idea—or, indeed, that it works—it may well be that it's worth a try, if only to see whether it might work under some conditions. The thing is that liberals—and I'm not a totally illiberal person, and I should make it reasonably clear that I'm not a right-wing conservative—tend to come down in favor of gun control because, I think, gun control avoids certain very uncomfortable issues. One is the ethnic issue, which is that the fear of crime is of black crime against white people, whereas the reality of crime, though nobody wants to admit it, is, if you look at the statistics, that it's mostly black crime against black people. And this is for the very good reason that black people cannot get jobs, they cannot get an education, they have no future, and under the present Administration they can see that things are going to get even worse. To address the real social issues is to see that we are not educating black children fast enough, and that even if we did educate them, we are not providing job incentives for them, and that we have allowed the drug thing to become so rooted that it is an ineradicable part of urban life."

7

IN NOVEMBER 1982 a referendum called Proposition 15 was put before the voters of California. It provided for a limit on privately held handguns, required all owners to register their weapons, and sought a jail term of six months for anyone found carrying an unlicensed and concealable firearm. California, with more than four million privately held handguns, was a fitting stage for what—after Morton Grove and Kennesaw—was billed as a decisive showdown in the national gun-control war. And, with so much at stake, both the gun lobby and the antigun movement threw themselves energetically into the Proposition 15 campaign. An N.R.A. spokesman called Proposition 15 "the most serious threat to firearms that has ever come down the road." And Nelson Shields, of Handgun Control, Inc., defined the importance of Proposition 15 in these terms: "If it succeeds, I predict it will . . . sweep across the country. If it fails, the invincibility of the gun lobby will be touted again."

Leading the fight for the proposition was a group called Californians Against Street Crime, which had secured more than six hundred thousand signatures, needed to place the proposition on the state ballot, and playing strong supportive roles were Handgun Control, Inc., the National Coalition to Ban Handguns, and hundreds of prominent Californians, a number of them from Hollywood. Though these organizations and individuals contributed just over $2 million to the proposition's campaign chest, that was a virtual drop in the bucket compared to the more than $6 million that the opposition raised and spent.

Organized as a coalition called Citizens Against the Gun Initiative, the opposition included Gun Owners of America, the California Rifle and Pistol Association, the Second Amendment Foundation, the Citizens Committee for the Right to Keep and Bear Arms, and the National Rifle Association. That aggregation also drew its share of support from Hollywood celebrities, one of whom, Roy Rogers, declared in the course of the campaign, "They'll have to kill me first to take my gun."

In that shootout, it was Proposition 15 that was killed:

Californians rejected it on November 2 by more than two to one. The gun lobby, having crushed its opponents in what had been billed as a confrontation of national gun forces, naturally declared that the vote in California was a vote for and about America, a vindication of the lobby's crusade to preserve for all Americans the right to own and use whatever guns they chose. On November 2, gun-control proposals had also been rejected in New Hampshire and Nevada. "In crucial votes in three states," Alan Gottlieb said, in interpreting the pro-gun triumph of that day, "Americans made it very plain that they will brook no interference with their right to keep and bear arms." He went on, "These votes clearly show that the antigun forces have been misrepresenting their polls and statistics for years. Where is their much proclaimed majority of Americans in favor of gun control? If they're out there, they certainly don't vote. . . . Why don't they listen to the will of the majority and just leave everybody alone?" According to the New York *Times,* John M. Snyder—the chief lobbyist for the Citizens Committee for the Right to Keep and Bear Arms—was sending out a Christmas card for 1982 that "showed Santa Claus with a sack full of pistols marked 'Morton Grove,' " and explained, ". . . . Santa was announcing his departure for California, a state that had just defeated a gun-control proposition."

That was adding insult to injury, for the gun-control forces had indeed been humiliated by their defeat in California. Victor Palmieri, a Los Angeles lawyer who had chaired the campaign to win acceptance for Proposition 15, confessed a feeling of embarrassment, and

described the failure as a sort of Bay of Pigs. Nelson
Shields had predicted at the outset that if Proposition
15 failed, "the invincibility of the gun lobby will be
touted again," and after the Proposition's defeat John
Phillips, another Los Angeles lawyer, said, "The N.R.A.
is going to make a lot of noise about this over the next
few years. I'm sad about that." In the noise that Alan
Gottlieb had already made, he was right about one
thing: if it's true that, as the polls have been saying for
years, a majority of Americans favor gun controls, then
"they certainly don't vote." And, considering the present mood and makeup of Congress, that is a dismal
omen for the future of gun-control legislation in the
United States. In assessing the cause of his movement's
defeat in California, Shields attributed none of it to the
apathetic voting habits of people who say they are
themselves in favor of gun control; apparently, he either overlooked that factor or was tacitly acknowledg-
ing a displeasing circumstance. Instead, he suggested
that the gun-control forces had been overpowered
by the superior financial muscle of the opposition.
Whether the three-to-one disparity in resources will be
narrowed in the near future seems doubtful. Shields did
not surrender his optimism, however—or did not surrender at all. For when he was asked if his movement
would fight another day, he replied, "You're damn
right we will, but not before we have the money in
hand."

Till that day arrives, the movement for gun control
might draw a degree of comfort from what John Hinck-

ley has been quoted as saying, from his place of incarceration in Washington: "If somebody like me can buy six Saturday Night Specials with ease, there is something drastically wrong. I'm considering my support to the the National Coalition to Ban Handguns."

The gun-control movement might also draw a measure of comfort from what the Supreme Court eventually decided about the case of Morton Grove. "March 7, 1983, was a day of infamy," the N.R.A.'s Warren Cassidy said when he learned of the final ruling of the United States Court of Appeals in Chicago. ". . . It was a day of darkness for the people of Morton Grove, for they have been robbed of a precious right enjoyed by all citizens of this country since the adoption of the Bill of Rights and the abolition of slavery. It was a day of darkness for the courts of this country. . . . And, perhaps most of all, it was a day of darkness for our United States Constitution as well. . . . No nation which fancies itself as having a government of laws, and not of men, can endure such deliberate suppression of the rights of the majority in order to satisfy the orchestrated clamor of a minority of political extremists. After agonizing deliberation, it now appears that the National Rifle Association, as the organization which has always championed the right of law-abiding citizens to own and use firearms, must seek to have this outrageous decision overturned by the United States Supreme Court." At the end of May the N.R.A. filed a petition before the Supreme Court asking the Court—according to *Reports from Washington*—to consider "whether the lower federal courts should have abstained from ruling on the

Morton Grove case . . . and whether the Second and
Fourteenth Amendments to the Constitution effectively prohibit state and local governments from enact-
ing gun bans." The Supreme Court remained silent on
the matter, however. In October of 1983 it, in effect,
dismissed the N.R.A. petition, by declining to rule on
the opinion delivered in March by the United States
Court of Appeals in Chicago. This was one of the few
serious setbacks the gun lobby had suffered in recent
years. From one of the most conservative courts in
decades, the lobby had hoped for a historic opinion,
upholding once and for all its own interpretation of the
Second Amendment. By its refusal to hear the case,
"the . . . Supreme Court is ducking the issue of gun
control," said *Point Blank*. "Its action underscores the
fact that the people no longer can rely on the courts to
protect them in the maintenance of their rights. The
people have to do that themselves, hopefully through
their elected representatives in Congress. That is why
pro-gun legislation now pending before Congress is so
important, indeed, necessary."

The most important piece of pro-gun legislation was,
of course, the McClure-Volkmer bill, which the President had promised to sign if it should be passed. But as
the pro-gun lobby regrouped to continue its struggle
against firearms control *it* could take encouragement
not only from the President's promise to sign the
McClure-Volkmer bill but also from the memory of an
address he had delivered to the hundred-and-twelfth
annual convention of the N.R.A., in May 1983. To a
gathering of about four thousand delegates, in Phoenix,

Arizona, Mr. Reagan said, "It does my spirit good to be with people who never lose faith in America, who never stop believing in her future, and who never back down one inch from defending the constitutional freedoms that are every American's birthright." He continued, "Being part of this group, you know that good organizations don't just happen. They take root in a body of shared beliefs. They grow from strong leadership with vision, initiative, and determination to reach great goals. And what you've accomplished speaks for itself—more than two and a half million members, and N.R.A.'s getting stronger every day." The President cited the defeat of Proposition 15 as proof of the N.R.A.'s growing strength. Then he said, "It is a nasty truth, but those who seek to inflict harm are not fazed by gun-control laws. I happen to know this from personal experience." He went on, "By the way, the Constitution does not say that government shall decree the right of the people to keep and bear arms. The Constitution says 'the right of the people to keep and bear arms shall not be infringed.' " The President said that "no group does more" than the N.R.A. "to promote gun safety and respect for the laws of this land," and he thanked the organization. "Still," he said, "we've both heard the charge that supporting gun owners' rights encourages a violent, shoot-'em-up society. But just a minute. Don't they understand that most violent crimes are not committed by decent, law-abiding citizens? They're committed by career criminals. Guns don't make criminals. Hard-core criminals use guns. And locking them up, the hard-core criminals up, and throwing away the key is the best gun-control law we could ever have."

Before the President spoke, people entering the hall had been closely checked by metal detectors. A sign posted near the entrance said, DUE TO PRESIDENTIAL SECURITY REASONS, NO GUNS, KNIVES, OR TEAR GAS WILL BE ALLOWED IN THE ASSEMBLY HALL. Perhaps it was odd that an organization of legal gun owners—and one so fond of President Reagan—should have found it necessary to issue such instructions to its membership. A resident of Suffield, Connecticut, said in a letter to the New York *Times:* "I note that metal detectors were used to screen the President's audience in Phoenix and that, naturally, no weapons of any type were allowed. Here we see at work essential hypocrisy: Gun control is utilized when the President makes a speech stating that he does not believe in gun control."

INDEX

Albright, Joseph, 81
Allen, Frederick Lewis, 66
America as a Civilization (Lerner), 72
American Humane Association, 37
Amory, Cleveland, 38
Anderson, Sherwood, 64–65
antihunting movement, 36–38
Audubon, 30

Bainbridge, John, 14–15
Beard, Michael, 90–92, 113–14
Biaggi, Mario, 105–7
Bijan handgun, 47–48
Boone, Daniel, 23
Booth, John Wilkes, 6, 49
Bradley, Ed, 83–84
Brady, James, 114
Breckinridge, John, 18–19
Brookhaven, New York, 102–4
Bryant, Bob, 16
Bryant, Will, 45
buffalo, 23–26
bullets, cop-killer, 101–7
Bureau of Alcohol, Tobacco and Firearms, U.S., 75
Burke, Steve, 102–4

California, Proposition 15 referendum in, 120–23, 126
Californians Against Street Crime, 121
Carter, Harlan, 97
Cashman, Neil, 110–11
Cassidy, Warren, 105, 124
cattle trade, 55–59
Cawelti, John G., 13

children, 11–12
as handgun owners, 83
media gun-play and, 64–71, 83–84
shootings by, 78–79
Chrisman, Henry, 61–62
Christian Science Monitor, 70
Citizens Against the Gun Initiative, 121
Citizens Committee for the Right to Keep and Bear Arms, 94–96, 101, 108–9, 121
Clarens, Carlos, 66
Clede, Bill, 100
Colt, Samuel, 51–54
revolvers made by, 49–56
Colt .45 Peacemaker, 41–42, 46, 50, 54–55
Congress, U.S., 70, 84–86, 89–90, 108–9
Constitution, U.S., Second Amendment to, 98–99, 107–9, 126
cowboys, 56–57, 61–62
cowtowns, 56–59
crime movies, 66–67
crime rate, 76–80, 86–88

D'Amato, Alphonse, 93–94
Deringer, Henry, Jr., 49
derringer, 49
Detroit, shooting in, 11, 81–82
Dickens, Charles, 8, 17–18, 59
duels, 17–19

Earp, Wyatt, 46, 58
Eron, Leonard D., 71

FBI Crime Reports, 75, 88–89
Federal Firearms Act of 1938, 85
Field and Stream, 4
Fields, Sam, 50
Firearm Owners Protection Act
  (proposed), 89–90
Friends of Animals, 37–38
Fund for Animals, 38

Gerbner, George, 70
Gilligan, Edmund, 35–36
Gottlieb, Alan, 95, 100–101, 122
*Great American Guns and
  Frontier Fighters* (Bryant), 45
gun collecting, 41–42
gun control, 85–127
  cop-killer bullets and, 101–7
  effectiveness of, 87–89, 119
  handguns as focus of, 100–101
  issues relevant to, 117–18
  legislation for, 85–86, 88–92
  as liberal issue, 116–17, 119–20
  local ordinances on, 109–14, 118,
    124–25
  mandatory gun ownership and,
    114–16
  organizations for, 90–94
  product-liability suits and, 113–14
  state propositions on, 120–23
Gun Control Act of 1968, 85–86,
  89, 98
gun manufacturers, 19
gun purchases, 14, 16, 81–83
guns:
  as American institution, 8–12
  culture built around, 19–22
  freedom won by, 16–17
  mandatory ownership of, 114–16
Guns & Ammo, 68, 100
Gun Week, 30, 116

Handgun Control, Inc., 90–94,
  96–97, 121
handguns, 45–60, 75–84
  ancestors of, 48–55
  children as owners of, 83
  designer, 47–48
  as focus of gun control, 100–101
  in frontier towns, 56–59
  as gifts from banks, 46–47
  image of, 13–14, 45–46

importation banned for, 86
  purchase conditions for, 81–83
  quantity of, 9, 75
  for self-protection, 77–80
Harris, Jean, 13–14
Hatch, Orrin, G., 108–9
Hickey, James, 101
Hickock, Wild Bill, 58–59
Hinckley, John, Jr., 6, 9–10, 13, 71,
  82, 114, 123–24
Hofstadter, Richard, 9, 22
Holloway, Carrol C., 45–46
Humane Society of the United
  States, 38
hunting, 4, 24–38
  atrocities of, 33–34
  as contest, 32–33
  illegal, 30
  interference with, 36–37
  rifles and, 24–26
  as right, 29
  spending on, 30
  as sport, 30–34
  unsettling memories from, 35–36
  as wildlife preservation aid,
    36–38
  as youthful rite of passage, 11–13

Indians, 23, 51–54
Ingram, George, 34–35
Iżaak Walton League, 37

Jackson, Andrew, 5
Johnston, Phil, 34

Kahn, Herman, 11–13
Kennedy, Edward, 89–91
Kennedy, John F., 5–6
Kennesaw, Georgia, 114–16
Kenny, Jerry, 105–6
Kentucky General Assembly, 10–11
Kentucky rifle, 23–24, 51–52
Korda, Michael, 116–20

Laredo *Times*, 97
Law Enforcement News, 105
lawmen, Western, 58–59
  in movies, 63
Lawrence, D. H., 76
Lerner, Max, 72
Life, 66, 68

Lincoln, Abraham, 5–6
Lingeman, Richard, 56–57

McClure, James, 89–90
McCullough, David, 27
McKinley, William, 6
Maniscalco, Arlene, 39–40
Man Kind? (Amory), 38
Martin Chuzzlewit (Dickens), 8, 17–18
Masterson, Bat, 63–64
Mock, Bob, 47
Monitor (Reports from Washington), 4–5, 96, 116, 124–25
Morton Grove, Ill., 109–14, 124–25
Mottl, Ron, 70
movies, 62–67, 72, 84
Moynihan, Daniel Patrick, 105–7

National Audubon Society, 37
National Coalition to Ban Handguns, 15, 90–92, 121
National Firearms Act of 1934, 85
National Institute of Mental Health, 69
National Rifle Association (NRA), 4–5, 37, 94, 96–99, 108, 113–14, 116–17, 121–27
California Proposition 15 and, 121
cop-killer bullets and, 101–7
history of, 97–98
as lobby, 96–99
local gun control ordinances and, 112, 124–25
political contributions from, 93–94
Presidents and, 4–5
size of, 96
National Shooting Sports Foundation, 11
National Wildlife Federation, 37
New England, gun culture and, 19–20
New England Journal of Medicine, 76
Newsweek, 7, 16
New York *Post*, 117
New York *Times*, 36, 39–40, 71, 79–80, 101–2, 115, 122

O'Connor, Jack, 33
Odessa, Texas, as U.S. murder capital, 15–16
O.K. Corral shootout, 46, 58–59
One-Shot Antelope Hunt, 31–32, 35
Only Yesterday (Allen), 66
Outdoor Writers Association, 37
outlaws, Western, 58

Pakzad, Bijan, 48
Palmieri, Victor, 122–23
Pennsylvania rifles, 22–23
Philadelphia *Inquirer*, 97
Pistolero, 4, 7
Point Blank, 116, 125
Poland, Solidarity and, 99
police, cop-killer bullets and, 101–7
Preiser, Gerald, 39
presidency, U.S., gun ownership and, 4–7
Presley, Elvis, 46
pro-gun movement, 76, 94–109, 120–23
cop-killer bullets and, 101–7
local gun control ordinances and, 112–13
size and power of, 94–96
Purdy, Darvin, 115
Putnam, Carleton, 25

Radecki, Thomas, 70–71
Reagan, Ronald:
assassination attempt against, 6, 9–10, 71, 114
gun ownership position of, 6–7, 86–88, 90, 126–27
on hunting, 4
NRA and, 4–5, 98, 125–27
rifle as gift from, 3
Regenstein, Lewis, 32
Reports from Washington, see Monitor
rifles, 22–26
hunting and, 24–26
repeating, 24
single shot, 23–24
Rights of Gun Owners, The (Gottlieb), 100
Robb, Charles, 104–5
Rodino, Peter, 89–91

Roosevelt, Theodore, 5–6, 26–29,
    63–64
Rossi, Peter, 87–88
Ruger, Bill, 6–7

Saturday Night Specials, 11, 81–82,
    86
Second Amendment Foundation,
    94–95, 121
settlers and pioneers, 20–24, 56–57
Sherrill, Robert, 81–82
Shields, Nelson (Pete), 92–93, 121,
    123
shootings, 8–10, 15–16, 59–60
    accidental, 78–80
    as American institution, 10–12
    by children, 78–79
    family, 78–80
    homicides from, 75–76
    as "life skill," 10
    media depictions of, 60, 63–72,
        83–84
    non-gun crime vs., 76
    quantity of, 75–76
    Westerns and, 63–66
Siegel, Alberta Engvall, 69–70
Small Town America (Lingeman),
    56–57
snubbies, 80–82
Snyder, John M., 122
South, guns in, 17
Spillane, Mickey, 13
Straits Times, 10
suicides, 78
Sullivan Law (New York State),
    88
Super-Americans, The
    (Bainbridge), 14–15
Supreme Court, U.S., 108, 124–25
survivalists, 40–41
Swat, 40–41

target shooting, 38–41
    growth of, 39
    survivalists and, 40–41
television, 68–71, 83–84
Texas, 14–17
    Colt revolvers in, 52–55
    Eastern view of, 61
    handgun purchases in, 82–83
    Texas Gun Lore (Holloway), 45–46
Texas Rangers, 51–54
Tocqueville, Alexis de, 17
toys, 68–69
Trilling, Diana, 13–14
trophy hunting, 4
Turley, Windle, 114
Turner, Frederick Jackson, 21
Twain, Mark, 78

Uzi submachine guns, 40–41

Van den Haag, Ernest, 101
Volkmer, Harold, 89–90

Walker, Samuel, 53–54
Wall Street Journal, 60
Warshow, Robert, 69
Watt, James, 31–32
Webb, Walter Prescott, 50–51,
    60–61
West, Old, 56–62
Westerns (movies), 62–66
Whalen, Philip, 21
Wildlife Legislative Fund, 37
wildlife preservation, hunting and,
    36–38
Winchester rifles, 24, 26
women, gun machismo and, 13–14
World Fast Draw Association, 10
Wright, James, 87–88

Zhao Jinglun, 14

ABOUT THE AUTHOR

JERVIS ANDERSON, a native of Jamaica and a graduate of New York University, has been a staff writer for *The New Yorker* since 1968. He is the author of *A. Philip Randolph: A Biographical Portrait* and *This Was Harlem: 1900–1950.*

His writings have also appeared in *Commentary*, the *New Republic*, the *New York Review of Books*, *American Scholar*, *Dissent*, and the *New York Times Book Review*.

He is a fellow of the American Society of Historians and lives on the Upper West Side of Manhattan.

The Ultimate iPad
Your Digital Life at Your Fingertips
James Floyd Kelly

Safari Books Online

FREE Online Edition

DISCARD

Your purchase of **The Ultimate iPad** includes access to a free online edition for 45 days through the **Safari Books Online** subscription service. Nearly every Que book is available online through **Safari Books Online**, along with thousands of books and videos from publishers such as Addison-Wesley Professional, Cisco Press, Exam Cram, IBM Press, O'Reilly Media, Prentice Hall, Sams, and VMware Press.

Safari Books Online is a digital library providing searchable, on-demand access to thousands of technology, digital media, and professional development books and videos from leading publishers. With one monthly or yearly subscription price, you get unlimited access to learning tools and information on topics including mobile app and software development, tips and tricks on using your favorite gadgets, networking, project management, graphic design, and much more.

Activate your FREE Online Edition at
informit.com/safarifree

STEP 1:   Enter the coupon code: VEUFGDB.

STEP 2:   New Safari users, complete the brief registration form.
           Safari subscribers, just log in.

If you have difficulty registering on Safari or accessing the online edition,
please e-mail customer-service@safaribooksonline.com

Addison Wesley   AdobePress   ALPHA   Cisco Press   FT Press FINANCIAL TIMES   IBM Press   Microsoft Press   New Riders   O'REILLY

Peachpit Press   PRENTICE HALL   Que   Redbooks   SAMS   SAS Publishing   vmware PRESS   WILEY   wrox